Dollmaking
for the first time®

Dollmaking
for the first time®

Miriam Gourley

Sterling Publishing Co., Inc.
New York
A Sterling/Chapelle Book

Chapelle, Ltd.

Jo Packham
Sara Toliver
Cindy Stoeckl

Editor: Karmen Quinney
Photography: Ryne Hazen for Hazen Photography
Photo Stylist: Suzy Skadburg
Art Director: Karla Haberstich
Copy Editor: Marilyn Goff
Graphic Illustrator: Kim Taylor
Staff: Kelly Ashkettle, Anne Bruns, Areta Bingham,
    Donna Chambers, Emily Frandsen, Lana Hall,
    Susan Jorgensen, Jennifer Luman, Melissa Maynard,
    Barbara Milburn, Lecia Monsen, Linda Venditti,
    Desirée Wybrow

Library of Congress Cataloging-in-Publication Data

Gourley, Miriam, 1951-
    Dollmaking for the first time/ Miriam Gourley.
        p. cm.
    Includes index.
    ISBN 1-4027-0726-6
    1. Dollmaking. I Title.
TT175.G6825 2004
745.592'21--dc22   2004003332

10 9 8 7 6 5 4 3 2 1

Published by Sterling Publishing Co., Inc.
387 Park Avenue South, New York, NY 10016
©2004 by Miriam Gourley
Distributed in Canada by Sterling Publishing
% Canadian Manda Group, One Atlantic Avenue, Suite 105
Toronto, Ontario, Canada M6K 3E7
Distributed in Great Britain by Chrysalis Books Group PLC, The
Chrysalis Building, Bramley Road, London W10 6SP, England
Distributed in Australia by Capricorn Link (Australia) Pty. Ltd.
P.O. Box 704, Windsor, NSW 2756, Australia
Printed in China
All Rights Reserved

Sterling ISBN 1-4027-0726-6

Every effort has been made to ensure that all information in this book is accurate. However, due to differing conditions, tools, and individual skills, the publisher cannot be responsible for any injuries, losses, and/or other damages which may result from the use of the information in this book.

Due to the limited amount of space available, we must print our patterns at a reduced size in order to give our patrons the maximum number of patterns possible in our publications. We believe the quality and quantity of our patterns will compensate for any inconvenience this may cause.

Write Us

If you have questions or comments, please contact:
    Chapelle, Ltd., Inc.,
    P.O. Box 9252, Ogden, UT 84409
    (801) 621-2777 • (801) 621-2788 Fax
    e-mail: chapelle@chapelleltd.com
    web site: chapelleltd.com

Table of Contents

Section 1:
Dollmaking Basics—10

Section 2:
Basic Techniques—42

Section 3:
Beyond the Basics—74

Introduction

Dollmaking has been a part of human interest since the early history of the world. The ancients sometimes made replicas of humans to be companions in the graves of their dearly departed. Dollmaking has gradually evolved to creating companions for children, and as a wonderful hobby and art form for adults.

When we are young, we fear little in our creativity, and some of the brightest and most expressive pieces of art are often the products of young minds. As we enter more social art settings, there are the inevitable comments, such as, "When you color, you need to stay within the lines," or "That's the wrong color for hair." It is when you throw caution to the wind, and decide that "there are no rules", that you can achieve a great deal of satisfaction in your dollmaking efforts.

In this book, and in other dollmaking venues, try to create dolls that live somewhere in your imagination. Moonlight's yellow face on page 77, wasn't for shock value, but because people's faces look like that in the light of the bright October moon, and their hair actually can look blue or even purple. The Primitive Angel on page 105 is a reflection of my bedroom upstairs in the Old Crow Farmhouse where I grew up. The color of her skin looks like it has aged over time, and her clothing reflects the look of the wallpaper on my bedroom walls. The Native American dolls, both the wooden and cloth varieties, are reminders of our frequent family trips into the reservations of Northern New Mexico, and the colors of the dirt, the sky, and the houses there.

Try to surround yourself with things that have meaning that tie into your beloved family and childhood. When you create dolls, make them special by interjecting bits of laughter, whimsy, love, and even sorrow. Collect bits and pieces that will lend a special feeling to your creations. Mix colors that speak to your soul, then read *Dollmaking for the First Time®* and learn the technical aspects of how to hook some of those elements together, to create wonderful dolls to give away or keep.

Miriam Gourley

How to Use this Book

For the person who is contemplating making dolls for their first time, this book provides a starting point to teach basic skills. *Dollmaking for the first time*® contains techniques and methods, complete with patterns and instructions, to get you thoroughly hooked on dollmaking. The more you practice, the more comfortable you will feel.

Section 1: Dollmaking Basics familiarizes you with the basic materials and tools for dollmaking, then you will step into pattern preparation and stitching techniques. You will learn all about making noses, arms, legs, faces, bodies, whether you are working on a cloth doll or a wooden one. You will be shown how to paint or stitch faces and make hair and clothing for your dolls.

Section 2: Basic Techniques contains instructions for six techniques that can be used on cloth and wooden dolls. If you are timid about starting, this section will soon put you at ease as you learn to create a very simple cloth doll, then a cloth doll with sculpted fingers. Other techniques will teach you how to create dolls from wooden materials.

Section 3: Beyond the Basics expands on the techniques learned in Section 2. Now that you have learned how to glue paper onto wood, sculpt and paint beautiful faces, make amazing hairstyles, and dress your dolls well, you will be introduced to several projects on which to practice your new skills. Some are all cloth, others are wood and paper. You will enjoy looking at the photographs and making your favorite—unless you can't decide, and have to make them all.

Various skills are taught in this book. Learning these techniques and how to apply them will inspire you to create beautiful dolls of your own. Feel free to change the colors of the paints and the fabrics and embellish the dolls to suit your tastes and imagination.

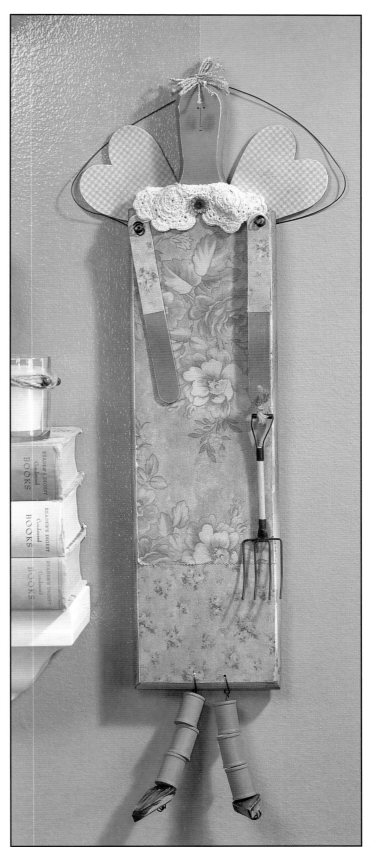

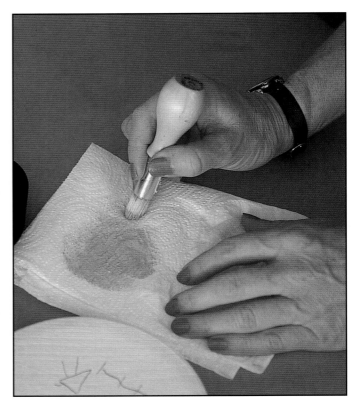

Section 1: Dollmaking Basics

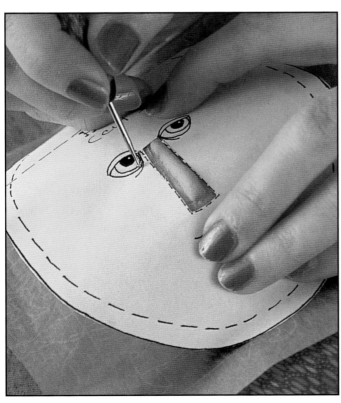

Needed Materials & Tools

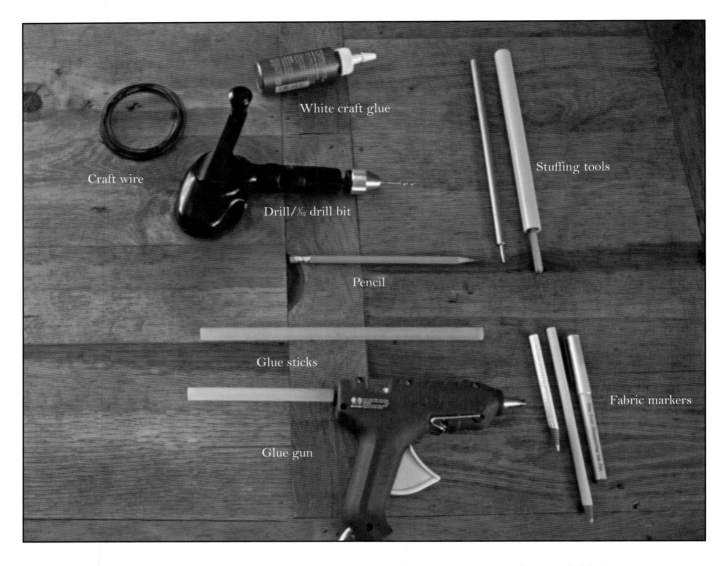

Craft wire

White craft glue

Stuffing tools

Drill/⅜₂ drill bit

Pencil

Glue sticks

Glue gun

Fabric markers

General Items

Most of the projects in this book require a few of the same materials and tools. The following items will be helpful in creating a doll whether it is cloth or wooden.

- **Craft scissors (not shown)**—used to cut out paper patterns and nonfabric items
- **Craft wire**—used to create hangers and attach arms and legs to wooden dolls
- **Drill/⅜₂ drill bit**—used to create holes in wooden pieces

- **Fabric markers**—used to mark fabrics
- **Iron/ironing board (not shown)**—used to press fabric items
- **Glue gun/glue sticks**—used to adhere clothing and embellishments in place
- **Pencil**—used to trace patterns and facial features and used to curl craft wire
- **Photocopier (not shown)**—used to enlarge and copy patterns
- **Stuffing tools**—used to push stuffing in place
- **White craft glue**—used to adhere clothing and embellishments in place
- **Wire cutters (not shown)**—used to cut wire

Painting Items

Painting items are used to create all of the doll faces in this book. The following painting items are suggested.

- **Acrylic paints**—used to paint body and faces
- **Brush tub**—used to rinse brushes
- **Mixing tray**—used to mix paints
- **Paper towels (not shown)**—used to blot paint
- **Sanding pad**—used to smooth rough surfaces on wood
- **Spray sealer (not shown)**—used to seal wooden pieces
- **Stylus**—used to transfer patterns and create facial features
- **Tack cloth**—used to remove dust from sanded items
- **Transfer paper (not shown)**—used to transfer doll patterns onto wood and cloth

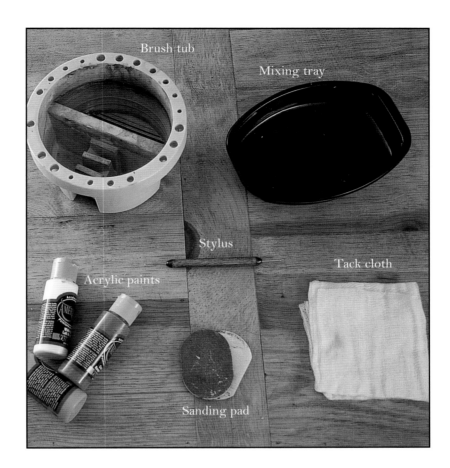

Paintbrushes

A long-bristled liner brush is great for painting fine lines such as eyelashes or eyelid lines. The liners with shorter bristles are great for adding details such as eye colors and lip colors.

The flat brushes are used to apply the base coat on either wooden or fabric dolls and to float color for shading. There are several widths that are useful, varying from a fairly wide brush (1") to narrow ones (½" and ¼").

Stiff round stencil brushes in various sizes can be used for dry-brushing.

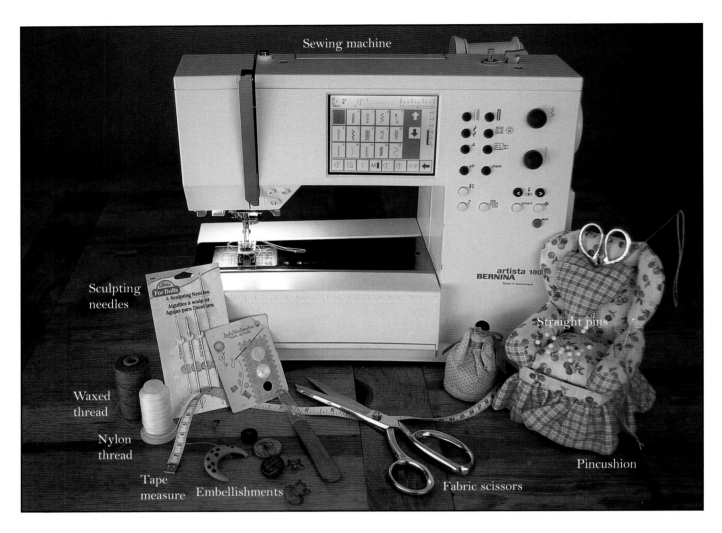

Sewing machine

Sculpting needles

Straight pins

Waxed thread

Nylon thread

Tape measure

Embellishments

Fabric scissors

Pincushion

Sewing Items

The art of making cloth dolls does not require a great deal of money—just some imagination and a few tools. In its simplest form, one can begin with as little as a few scraps of cloth, some stuffing, a basic sewing kit, and a work surface. Once you get hooked, you will probably want to invest in some equipment, including a good sewing machine. Try several machines, talk to those who use them a lot, and pick the best one you can afford.

• **Embellishments**—used to decorate doll
• **Embroidery needles (not shown)**—used to create decorative stitches on clothing
• **Nylon thread**—used to attach button joints to arms and legs

• **Pincushion**—used to store straight pins, quilting pins, and needles
• **Quilting thread (not shown)**—used to sculpt fingers, nose, and toes
• **Sculpting needles**—used to sculpt fingers, toes, facial features, and make button joints
• **Sewing machine and thread**—used to sew body pieces and clothing. A sewing machine is used for all stitching unless otherwise indicated.
• **Sewing needle and thread (not shown)**—used for all hand-stitching unless otherwise indicated
• **Sharp fabric scissors**—used to cut only fabric items
• **Straight pins**—used to hold fabric together for stitching
• **Tape measure**—used to measure fabric before cutting
• **Waxed thread**—used to attach button joints to arms and legs

Polyester stuffing

Sewing thread

Fabrics

Cloth Doll Materials

Fabrics, polyester stuffing, and sewing thread are the basic components of a cloth doll. The doll body is usually made from muslin, sometimes tea-dyed to give the effect of antique fabric. There are no hard-and-fast rules for making doll bodies; they can be made from any color or pattern of fabric. Muslin can also be painted any desired color. Fabric is a wonderful medium as it can be shaped with various sculpting methods. The cloth dolls are filled with polyester stuffing, which is loose and airy.

Hair Materials

There are many wonderful fibers that can be used for hair in doll making. Embroidery flosses and metallic threads can be used. Any kind of wool roving can be braided, curled, or used directly from the package. Some wool roving is combed, and some is braided onto twine (called wool crepe), then removed to leave curly strands of doll hair. There are many interesting yarns, including some wonderful new fibers sold in scrapbooking sections of the craft stores.

Wool fleece

Textured yarn

Wool fleece

Carded yarn

Acrylic yarn

Metallic thread

Curling wool crepe

Wooden Doll Materials

Making wooden dolls and dressing them with paper or fabric is a wonderful adventure. A visit to the craft store will yield many useful items for doll making. Wooden spools, clothespins, paddles, beads, and craft sticks can be purchased for creating a doll. A doll can be created by using a wooden clock for the body and adding a head, arms, and legs from spools.

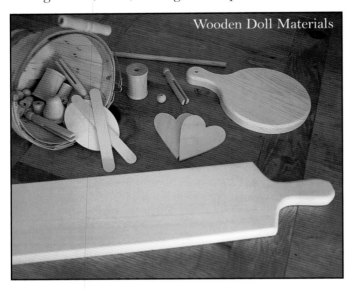

Wooden Doll Materials

Preparing the Patterns

There are three types of patterns used in this book. One type is a sewing pattern as shown at the right. All sewing patterns are marked with necessary information such as openings, fold placements, etc. Sewing patterns that use seam allowances will include a broken line inside the solid line. Unless otherwise indicated, these sewing patterns have a ¼" seam allowance.

Leave open to turn

Head Back
(cut 1)

Sewing Pattern
with Seam
Allowance

The second type of pattern is a face pattern as shown at the right. Face patterns are transferred onto wooden dolls.

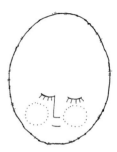

Face Pattern

The third type of pattern is a combination pattern as shown at the lower right. This type of pattern is a combination of a sewing pattern and a face pattern.

Use the following steps to prepare the patterns in this book:

1. Enlarge all patterns 200% on photocopier machine unless otherwise indicated.

2. Using craft scissors, cut out patterns to use as templates.

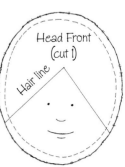

Head Front
(cut 1)

Hair line

Combination
Pattern

Making a Cloth Doll

Sculpting the Fingers

1. Sew body pieces, following individual project instructions. Before stuffing arm, use a pencil to mark stitching lines for fingers.

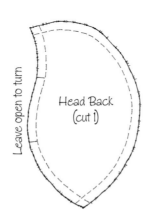

2. Topstitch along penciled lines, backstitching at the beginning and end to prevent unraveling.

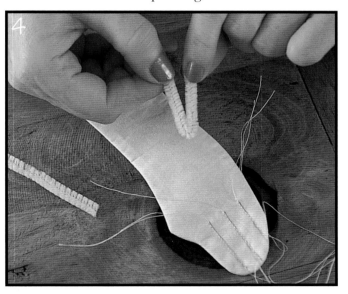

3. Using wire cutters, cut a piece from pipe cleaner twice the length of each pencil mark and add ⅛" for each finger.

4. Fold pipe cleaner in half and insert into finger with folded end at tip of finger.

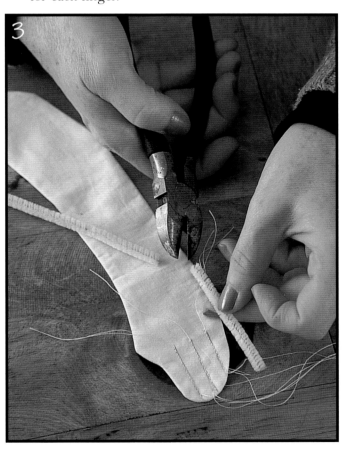

5. Repeat Steps 3–4 until all fingers have been sculpted.

6. Stuff the arm.

Sculpting the Toes

1. Cut pattern from doubled fabric, with right sides together. Sew front and back leg seams, leaving toes open. Clip along curves.

2. Pin the toe area together, matching the seams and the raw edges.

4. Turn leg right side out. Using pencil, mark stitching lines for toes. Stuff leg firmly.

3. Sew across opening, rounding corners a little.

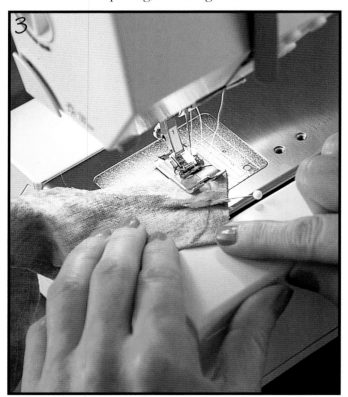

5. Insert sculpting needle with quilting thread into side of foot, exiting from the mark closest to the big toe. Leave a 2" tail.

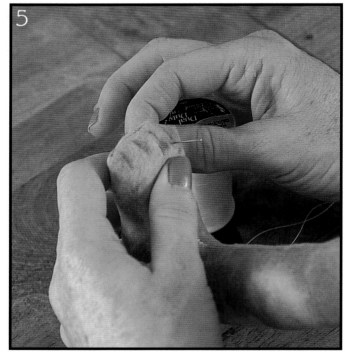

6. Make a tiny stitch to secure thread.

8. Make a small knot at exit point and reenter exit point, moving needle so it will exit from next toe mark.

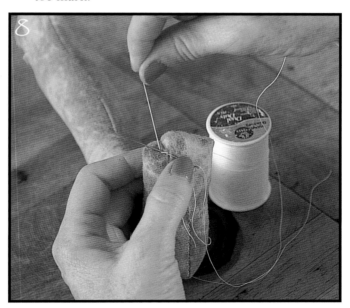

7. Reinsert needle into stitch, exiting from bottom of foot. Bring thread around front of foot, back into first stitch, and out bottom of foot, again.

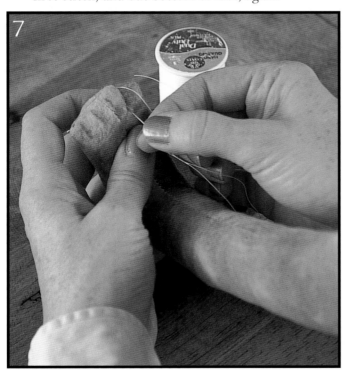

9. Repeat Steps 6–8, until all toes have been sculpted. Make final knot and bury thread, exiting from side of foot. Trim thread tails close to foot.

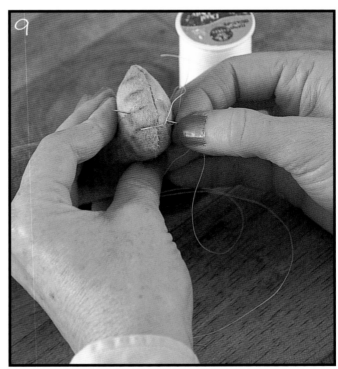

Stuffing the Doll Pieces

1. Remove a small amount of polyester stuffing from bag, and stretch stuffing a little to fluff it.

2. Insert stuffing into opening of stitched piece.

3. Using stuffing tool, push stuffing to furthest end of piece. If piece is fairly large, push stuffing to edges of piece before filling in center.

4. Add more stuffing, using stuffing tool to push firmly in place. *Note: If the piece looks lumpy, more stuffing may need to be inserted and pushed firmly in place.* Hand-stitch closed.

Sculpting the Nose

1. When head is stuffed firmly, place transfer paper and face pattern onto doll face. Using stylus, transfer nose. Using a pencil, define nose lines.

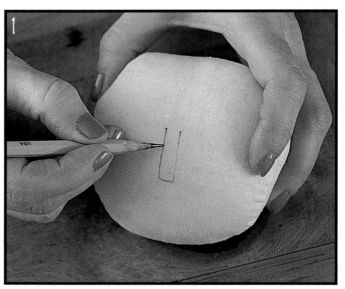

2. Thread sculpting needle with quilting thread. Do not make a knot at the end.

3. Insert needle into left side of head, leaving a 1" tail. Exit needle from upper-left side of nose.

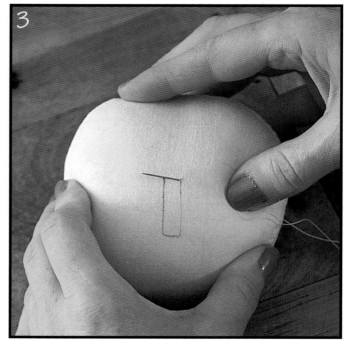

4. Take a small stitch, near exit point, to secure thread.

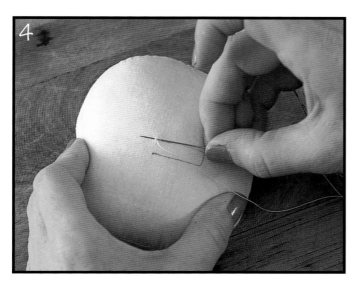

5. Reinsert needle into the upper-left side of nose, exiting from the upper-right side. Slide needle under some of the stuffing, to make nose more three-dimensional.

6. Insert needle a fraction of an inch below exit point on right, and exit needle on left side, just under first stitch.

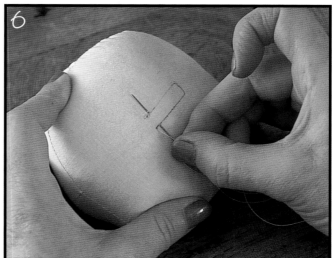

7. Repeat this procedure, working down along nose to lower end.

8. To finish bottom of nose, make a small stitch at left side, exit midway up on right, and repeat until you stitch lower-left side.

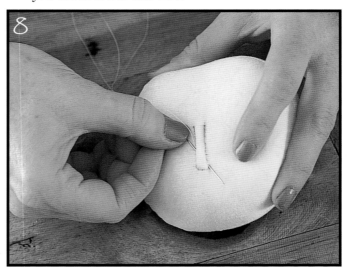

9. Repeat this procedure, stitching lower-right side and exiting from left side of nose.

10. Exit needle from the side of the head. Clip threads close to head. Stitch opening closed.

Attaching the Arms

1. Hand-stitch arm opening closed.

2. Whipstitch upper end of arm to shoulder with quilting thread.

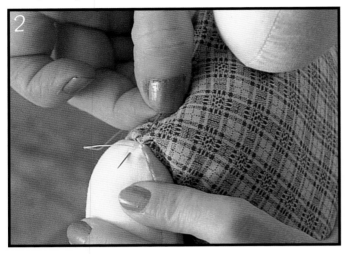

Attaching the Legs

Inserted Legs

1. Make certain upper 1" of leg is left unstuffed.

2. Leave body unstuffed until after legs are stitched in place. Pin legs to right side of top layer on lower body. If legs have toes, make certain they are pointed toward face.

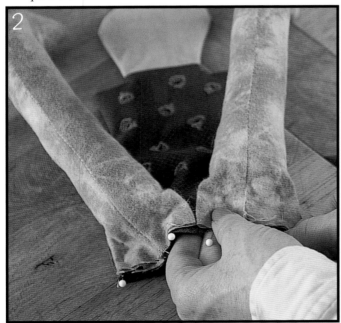

3. Sew legs to body, ¼" from raw edges. *Note: Hand-stitch legs, if the opening to the body is too small to machine stitch.*

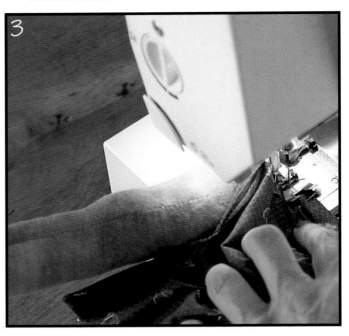

4. Stuff body, then hand-stitch opening closed, with raw edges tucked inside.

Button-on Joints

In order to "position" a doll, button joints are necessary. Use a long sculpting needle and a long piece of waxed thread, such as upholstery thread, and two large buttons.

1. Insert sculpting needle with waxed thread into button, then into upper leg (see individual pattern for placement). Leave a 6" tail.

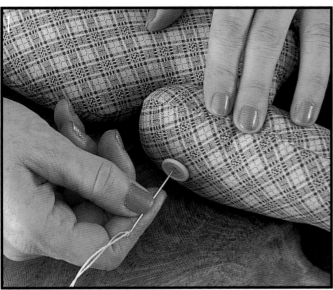

2. Insert needle into hip area, exiting from the opposite hip.

3. Continue through remaining leg and button. Insert needle back into opposite hole in button.

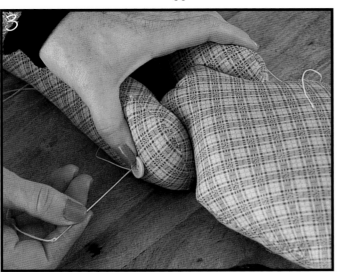

4. Continue back through leg, hips, opposite leg, and button.

5. Remove needle from thread, pull thread taut (but avoid bunching up the body), and knot. Trim ends of thread about ¼" from button. *Note: This method can be used for jointed arms.*

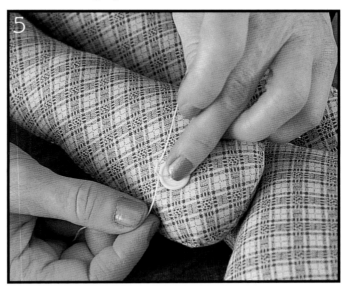

Author's Tips:
• Have someone assist when doing button-on joints. Have them hold the doll together while you are pushing the needle through the hips and lower body.
• Use flat buttons with two holes for button-on joints rather than shank buttons.
• As an alternative to button joints, whipstitch legs to hips with quilting thread. Be certain to pin legs in place first.
• Be certain to stand the doll on the table and pin legs to the lower body before sewing, so the feet will be even.

Transferring Facial Features onto Cloth

Flat Face Transfer

1. Transfer facial features by placing the pattern against a window or computer screen. Place the fabric over the pattern.

2. Using a pencil, transfer facial features onto muslin. *Note: This method was used on the Native American Doll shown below.*

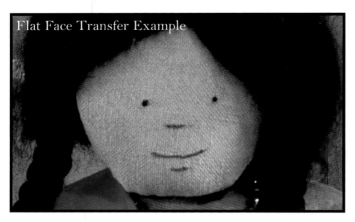

Flat Face Transfer Example

Sculpted Face Transfer

1. Layer face pattern on transfer paper, waxy side down, and cut out nose.

2. Place pattern with transfer paper onto doll face (previously base-coated). Using stylus, transfer facial features.

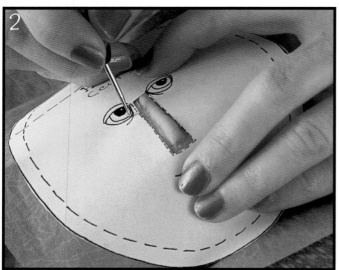

3. Remove pattern and transfer paper. Check to see if marks are dark enough, or if the face is centered appropriately. *Note: If using transfer paper that is water-removable, you can simply start over if you make a mistake.*

Note: This method was used on Josephine shown below.

Sculpted Face Transfer Example

Making a Wooden Doll

Preparing the Wood

1. Prepare wood, by using fine-grit sanding pad to smooth rough surfaces. Using tack cloth, wipe off dust.

2. Using flat brush and even strokes, base-coat wood with acrylic paint, following project instructions.

3. When paint is completely dry, lightly sand painted surface until it is completely smooth.

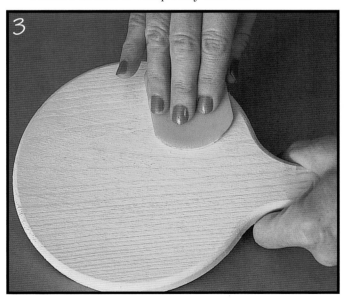

4. Using tack cloth, wipe off dust.

Covering the Wood with Decorative Paper

1. Place wood piece on paper. Using pencil, trace shape of piece onto paper. *Note: If wood is beveled, use a pencil to draw on the wood around the perimeter of the area to be papered and photocopy shape to use as a pattern. This method can also be used with fabric.*

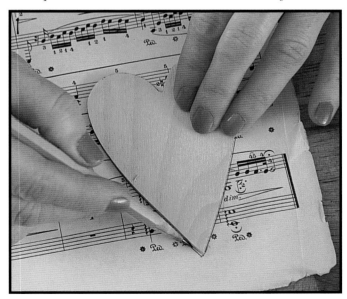

2. Cut or tear paper to fit wood. Torn paper makes the piece look a little more aged.

3. Apply a small amount of white craft glue to wood. Using fingers, spread glue evenly. Make certain glue goes to the edge of the surface to be papered.

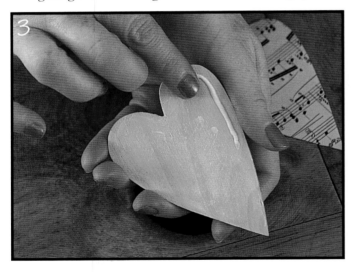

4. Place paper onto the surface, and smooth with a dry, clean cloth. Let dry thoroughly. If desired, sand the edges of the paper. *Note: If using fabric, adhere fabric with right sides up.*

5. Spray edges and back of wood with sealer. *Note: To "age" the doll, spray with wood-toned glossy stain. If you like a cleaner look, spray with clear sealer.*

Transferring Facial Features onto Wood

1. Place transfer paper, waxy side down, on wood surface.

2. Position pattern on transfer paper. Using stylus, press along lines of design to be painted. Avoid pressing too hard, as the lines will be too dark, and will be more difficult to cover with paint.

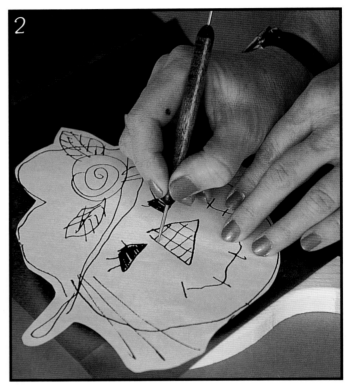

3. Paint details per individual project instructions. Let dry.

Author's Tip:
• Practice drawing an original face for your doll. Look at magazines and craft books for ideas, then use transfer paper to transfer your design to the doll's face.

Securing Wooden Arms & Legs onto Body

Arms

1. Using drill, make holes through upper arm and shoulder.

2. Using wire cutters, cut a length of wire. Wind one end around a pencil.

3. Push straight end of wire into hole in arm, then into shoulder hole, exiting from back.

4. Wind wire around pencil, clip off any excess wire.

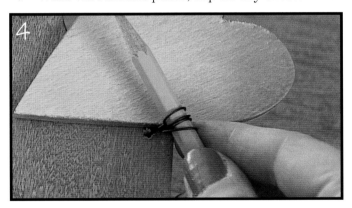

Note: You can also use hot glue to attach arms to the paddle dolls, if you do not want them to be able to move.

Legs

1. Using drill, make two holes at bottom edge of paddle and through any embellishments that you want to attach for legs and shoes.

2. Paint wooden embellishments to match clothing. Insert wire into holes at lower edge of paddle.

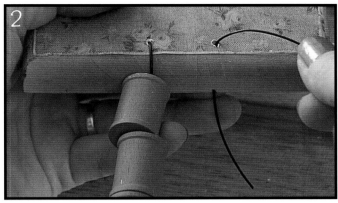

3. Twist wire to secure.

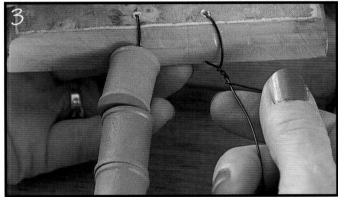

4. Thread embellishments onto wire.

5. Insert end of wire into back of hole of final embellishment. Bring wire through embellishment. Curl ends so final embellishment is snug against bottom of leg embellishment.

Painting Techniques

Floating Method

1. Using flat brush, dip brush into water and blot brush onto paper towel.

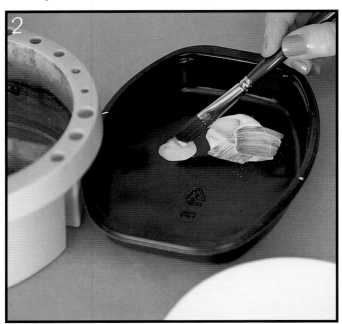

2. Dip one corner of brush into paint.

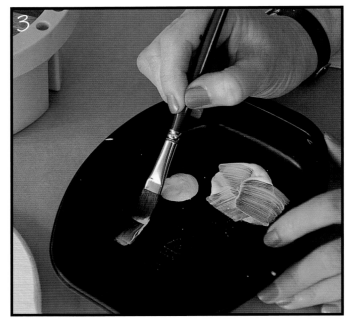

3. Brush back and forth two or three times on a palette to even out paint. Be careful to keep paint on one corner.

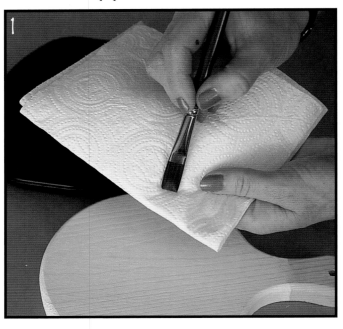

4. Apply paint, following individual project instructions. Apply paint on the outer edge of design. If done correctly, the color is deepest on the outer edge, fading gradually toward the other side of brush.

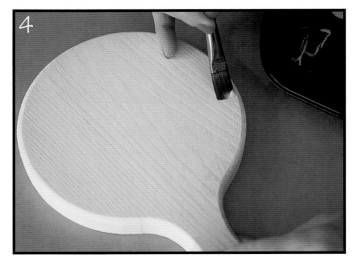

Antiquing Methods
Gel-based Stain

1. After final painting is thoroughly dry, brush on a gel-based stain with even strokes.

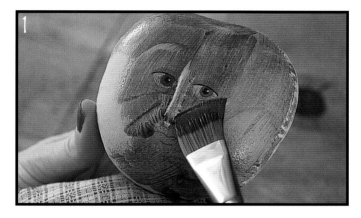

2. Using paper towel, remove excess stain. Remove as much or little as desired, depending on how you want the doll to look.

Acrylic Paint

1. When antiquing an unpainted fabric doll, first spray finished doll with water.

2. Mix burnt-umber paint with water to make a wash. Brush wash onto doll.

Crackle Medium

1. To add a crackled finish to the painted antiqued look, brush on crackle medium. When crackle medium is dry, brush on gel-based stain. Using paper towel, remove excess stain. Let dry.

2. Spray with sealer.

Painting the Face
Noses

Most doll noses are not painted a different color than the face. The exception in this book is the Scarecrow Annie doll on page 70.

Cheeks

To paint cheeks, a method called dry-brushing is used. A stiff brush is necessary, such as a round stencil brush. If the cheek area is small, use a small brush.

1. Dip brush into acrylic paint.

2. Rub brush onto paper towel until paint begins to look like powder.

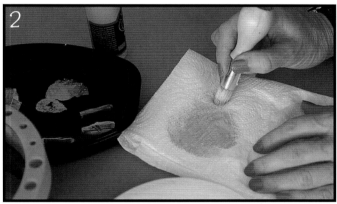

3. Apply color to cheek area, in a circular motion, until degree of desired color is achieved.

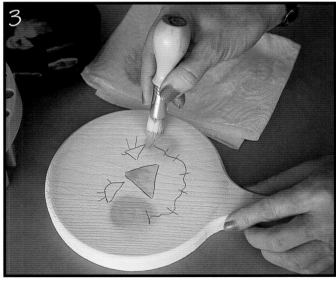

Simple Eyes

Below are three different methods for creating simple eyes.

Method # 1

1. Using stylus dipped in black or dark brown paint, dot eyes.

Method # 2

1. Using fine-tipped permanent marker, draw eyes.

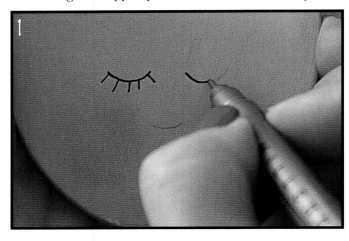

Method # 3

1. Create eyes with shapes painted black, and simple highlights added with a lighter color paint. For example, Scarecrow Annie's eyes shown below.

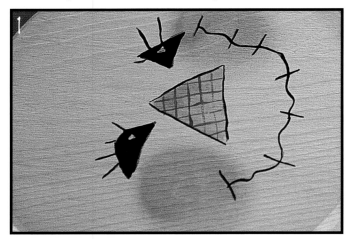

Detailed Eyes

1. Using liner brush, paint iris.

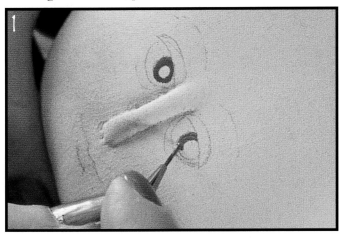

2. Paint upper eyelid. *Note: Rinse liner brush with water when using a different color of paint.*

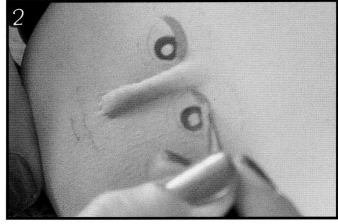

3. Paint lower eyelid.

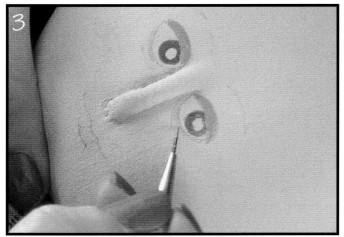

4. Paint pupil.

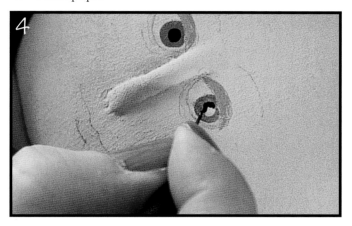

5. Paint whites of eyes. Using liner brush or stylus, apply highlight in pupil with paint.

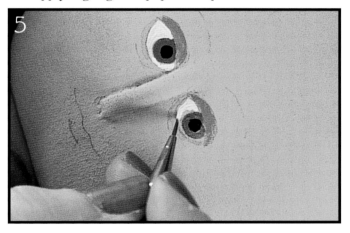

Simple Lips

Lips can be created with a basic shape or dots. Below are two different methods for creating simple lips.

Method #1

1. Using stylus, apply three dots of paint—two on top, and one on the bottom.

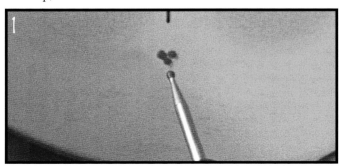

Method #2

1. Using liner brush, draw heart shape for mouth with paint. *Note: A red fine-tipped permanent marker may also be used to create lips.*

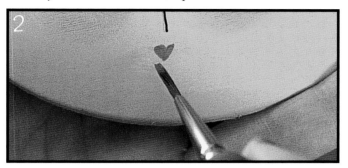

Detailed Lips

1. Using liner brush, paint thin horizontal line through center of lips to sperate lips. *Note: This line has several curves.*

2. Dilute desired color of paint for lips with water. Apply several layers of paint to lips, starting out very pale

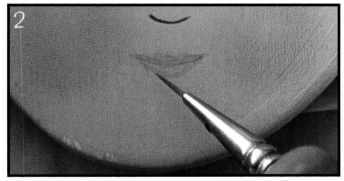

3. Build color on desired parts of the lips.

Creating the Hairdos

Curly Wool Roving

1. Using craft glue, adhere curly wool roving directly onto head, starting in front and ending in back. Pull it apart slightly, and stretch it as you wind the hair around the head.

2. If less curl is desired, curly wool roving can be slightly straightened. Using an iron, steam the roving to slightly straighten.

Wool Roving

1. Using craft glue, adhere wool roving directly onto head. Start at lower neck, working in layers toward top of head.

Wool Crepe

1. Using craft glue, adhere wool crepe directly onto head. Start at lower neck, working in layers toward top of head.

Embroidery Floss, Thread & Yarn

1. Cut several strands of chosen fiber. Using another strand, tie together at center. Using craft glue, adhere knot onto top of head. Cut ends short, letting strands hang down at sides. Braid ends, or tie a ponytail on side, and embellish as desired.

2. Adhere a hat, crown, or ribbon over top of head covering knot.

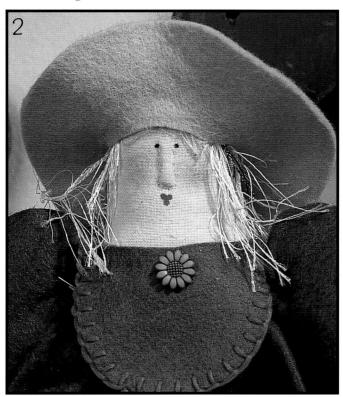

Nonfiber items

1. Hot-glue nonfiber items to top and back of head, such as inverted rusty-tin hearts shown below.

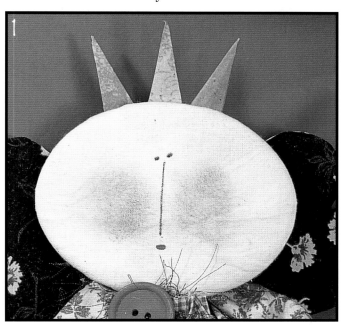

2. Make a paper cone hat. Wrap metallic thread around base.

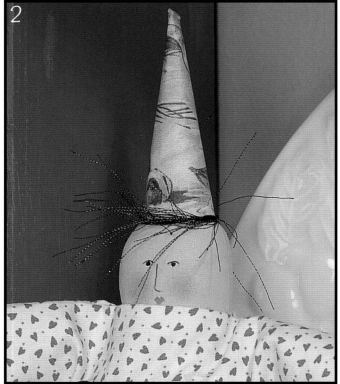

Making the Clothing

Bloomers

1. Cut bloomers from fabric, using individual project dimensions.

2. For leg openings, cut an inseam in two layers, directly at center.

3. Sew side seams, then inseam. Clip crotch seam allowance close to the stitching. Turn right side out and press seam allowance open.

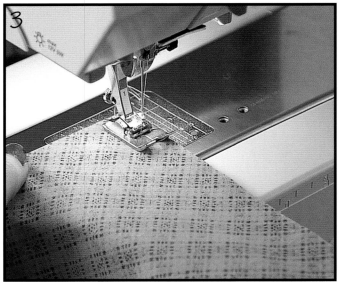

4. Press under a hem, if desired, or leave leg openings frayed.

5. Place bloomers on doll. Gather-stitch along waistline to fit doll. Pull stitches taut and knot.

T-dress

1. Cut two rectangles for T-dress from fabric, using individual project dimensions for width (w) and length (l).

2. With right sides together, sew along top edge (w), leaving a neck opening large enough to let head slip through. Press seam allowances open.

3. Cut away excess fabric from sides, using individual project dimensions for sleeves. *Note: Fabric should be in a T-shape.*

4. Sew underarm and side seams, clipping at corners. Turn right side out and press.

5. Hem lower edge, if desired. If the dress is short and will be tucked inside a skirt, hemming is unnecessary. *Note: You can also make a slit part way up the front, to leave open to create a jacket.*

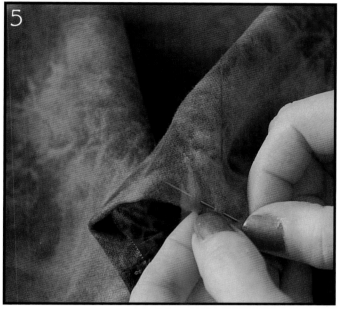

6. Place T-dress on doll and hand-stitch neck opening close to neck.

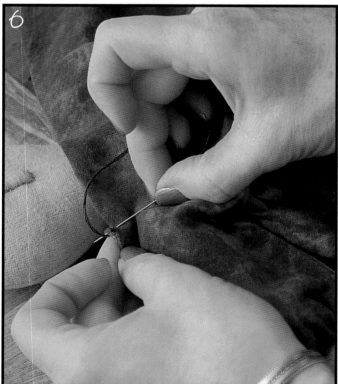

Gathered T-dress

1. Refer to **T-dress**, Steps 1–2 on page 34.

2. Measure the width of the sleeve opening. At the bottom of the sleeve opening, cut sleeve length, through both layers of fabric, plus 1".

3. Gather-stitch along lower edge of sleeve, and fold up gather to match raw edges of dress. Stitch gathers to upper part of dress.

4. Gather along lower edge of sleeve line, and fold up gathers to match raw edges of sleeve. Stitch gathers to upper part of dress sleeve.

5. With right sides together, sew sleeve and side seams. Clip corners, and turn right side out.

6. Finish dress. Refer to **T-dress**, Steps 4–6 on page 35.

Skirts

1. Cut or tear lower skirt from fabric, using individual project dimensions. Sew side seam with right sides together, matching raw edges.

2. Press seam allowances open.

3. Cut or tear upper skirt from fabric, using individual project dimensions.

4. Place skirt(s) on doll. Gather-stitch both skirt waists to fit doll.

5. If the skirt has a waistband, cut waistband, using individual project dimensions. Press under raw edges, wide enough and long enough to fit around the doll waistband (add a seam allowance). Place waistband around doll, centering opening in back. Hand-stitch in place. *Note: Ribbon can also be used to cover raw edges.*

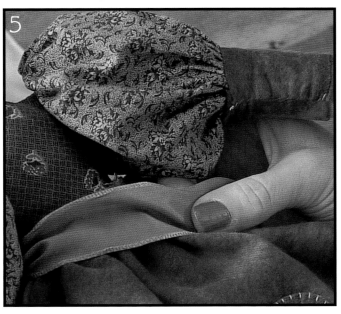

Fancy Sleeves

1. Cut sleeves from fabric, using individual project dimensions. With right sides together, sew along short edges. Press seam allowances open.

2. Turn right side out, and gather-stitch both unstitched edges. Place on arm.

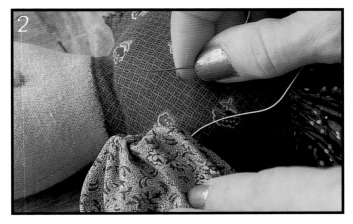

3. Tuck raw edges inside at top part of sleeve. Pull threads to gather. Hand-stitch in place at both ends.

4. Sew a piece of fabric into a tube shape. Turn right side out and press. Place on raw edge of sleeve.

5. Tuck the tube edges inside and hand-stitch onto the raw sleeve edges.

Pillowcase Sleeves

1. Cut pillowcase sleeves from fabric, using individual project dimensions. With right sides together, sew along straight portion of one side edge.

2. Press seam allowance open.

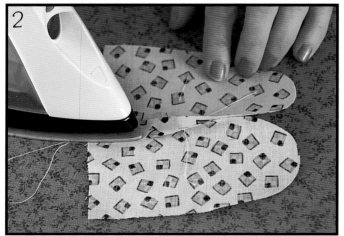

3. Cut binding from desired fabric for edge of sleeve, 2" x total width of stitched sleeve.

4. With right side of binding to wrong side of sleeve, sew binding to edge of sleeve, a scant ½" from raw edges.

5. Fold raw edge of binding inward a scant ¾" and press.

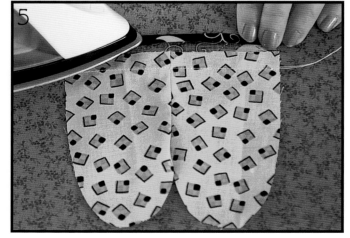

6. Bring folded edge of binding around to right side of sleeve and topstitch.

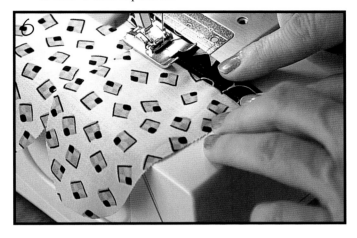

7. With right sides together, sew sleeve seam to bottom of binding. Turn right side out and press.

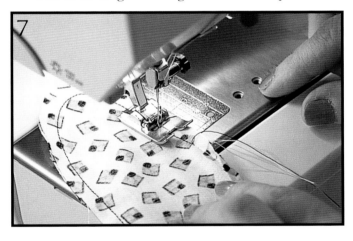

8. Insert stuffed arm into sleeve and hand-stitch arm and sleeve to shoulder of body.

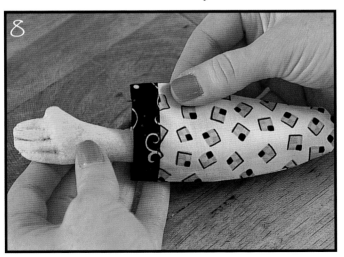

Collars

Felt

1. Center and cut a hole in a piece of felt for neck. Trim collar to desired shape.

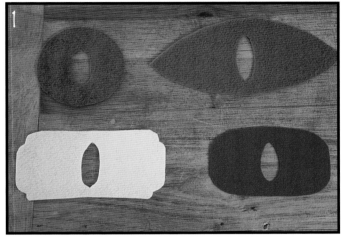

2. Trim edge by whipstitching or buttonhole-stitching edge of collar with a contrasting color of embroidery floss.

3. Embellish collar as desired.

Lace Doily

Method # 1
1. Cut an oval shape from lace doily for neck opening.

Method # 2
1. Cut a doily in half, fold under raw edges and adhere onto front of neck for collar.

Fabric Scrap

1. Place a cut or torn strip of fabric around neck.

2. Knot fabric or stitch on a button to make a scarf-type collar.

Embellishments

Add almost anything you can think of to embellish the clothing. Hand-stitch with embroidery floss, silk ribbons, or beads. Small charms, antique bits of clothing or lace, and other findings are sometimes the perfect embellishment.

Embellishments

Paint wooden buttons to match, lightly sand, to look old, and adhere or hand-stitch to clothes. Felt can be cut into any motif desired, then appliquéd onto the surface of the clothing, using small even stitches or large primitive ones.

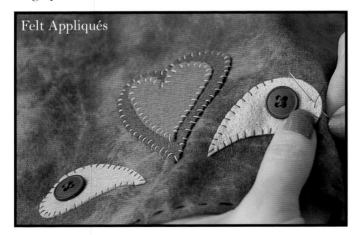
Felt Appliqués

Braid fabric strips together, then hand-stitch or adhere onto clothing. Braided fabric strips can be wrapped around the head for a funky hat.

Making the Shoes

At their simplest, shoes can be painted onto the doll's foot, such as the Shaker Doll's shoes on page 53. Shoe styles are cut from three basic pieces: a sole, a heel covering, and a toe covering. The toe covering can be pointed or rounded in the front, and the sole must be cut to match the foot's shape.

Making a Shoe Pattern

1. Using pencil, draw shape of foot onto paper for sole. Add ¼" seam allowances. Using craft scissors, cut out.

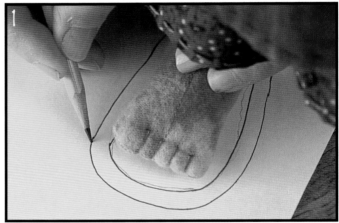

2. Drape a piece of muslin over foot to determine shape of toe covering. Using fabric scissors, cut front edge to match front of sole.

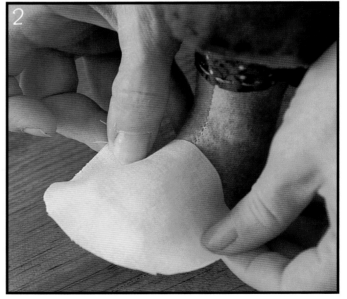

3. Drape another piece of muslin around back. Cut to fit heel covering. *Note: The heel covering is almost a U-shape.*

Making the Moccasins

1. Create a moccasin, using the three basic pieces for a shoe. Cut heel covering 5" high. Stitch toe covering to front half of sole. *Note: The heel covering on a moccasin is cut higher than a regular shoe so that fringe can be created.*

2. Fold heel covering down ½" above bottom edge, then stitch close to top folded edge for a casing. Clip excess length every ¼" up to stitching for fringe.

3. Bend heel around back of sole in a "U" shape. Overlap edges of toe covering.

4. Whipstitch heel covering to back of sole.

41

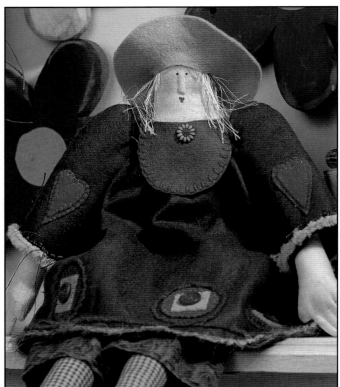

Section 2: Basic Techniques

1
technique

What you need to get started:

Materials & Tools

- General Items on page 12
- Painting Items on page 13
- Sewing Items on page 14
- Acrylic paints: flesh; rose
- Bits of lace
- Black fine-tipped permanent marker
- Embroidery floss: burnt orange; silver metallic
- Fabric scraps for dress, underskirt, apron
- Muslin scraps for body
- Paintbrushes: flat; tiny stencil
- Silver button
- Yarn for hair

How do I make a simple cloth doll?

This doll's body is all one piece. She is created by tracing and stitching the pattern onto muslin, then the doll is sewn, cut out, and stuffed. Simply transfer the face pattern provided onto the doll's head, using transfer paper and a stylus and use the paint colors provided to create her face. Her clothing is basic skirt with matching sleeves. Bits of lace and a silver button embellish the outfit. Embroidery floss is used to create the hairdo.

Simple Lucinda

Here's how:

Creating the Doll

1. Using **Simple Lucinda's** pattern on page 47, prepare patterns. Refer to **Preparing the Patterns** on page 16.

2. Trace and stitch pattern, using following technique.

   a. Place pattern on doubled fabric with right sides together.

   b. Using pencil, trace around outside edge of pattern. *Note: The pencil marks will be your stitching lines.*

Continued on page 46.

45

Continued from page 44.

c. Stitch along pencil lines, leaving openings as indicated on pattern piece.

d. Using fabric scissors, trim seam allowance to ⅛". Turn piece right side out.

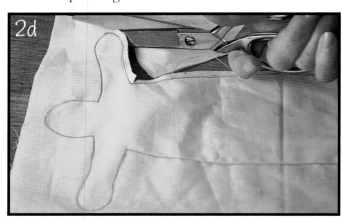

3. Using stuffing tool, stuff arms approximately halfway to shoulder. Refer to **Stuffing the Doll Pieces** on page 20.

4. Topstitch shoulder seams. See **Top-stitch** on page 47.

5. Stuff head and body. Hand-stitch opening closed. See **Diagram A** at right.

Diagram A

Painting the Doll

1. Using flat brush, base-coat head and hands with flesh paint.

2. Using stencil brush, dry-brush cheeks with rose paint. Refer to **Cheeks** on page 29.

3. Transfer face onto doll. Refer to **Sculpted Nose Transfer** on page 24. *Note: This doll does not have a sculpted face, but the head has been base-coated so, the Sculpted Face Transfer is necessary.*

4. Using marker, trace eyes, eyebrows, and nose on doll.

5. Using liner brush, paint lips with rose paint. Refer to **Simple Lips** on page 31.

Dressing the Doll

1. Using fabric scissors, cut 6½" x 14½" piece from desired fabric for lower skirt. Cut 5¾" x 14½" piece from desired fabric for upper skirt. Make skirts. Refer to **Skirts** on pages 36–37.

2. Cut 2¾" x 10" rectangle from desired fabric. Make fancy sleeves. Refer to **Fancy Sleeves** on pages 37–38.

3. Adhere pieces of lace and button onto bodice.

Creating a Hairdo

1. Make pom-pom hairdo with burnt-orange floss and metallic floss. Refer to **Embroidery Floss, Thread & Yarn** on page 33. See **Diagram A** below.

Diagram A

2. Clip loops to ⅛" from knot on each side. Adhere onto top of head.

Simple Lucinda's Back View

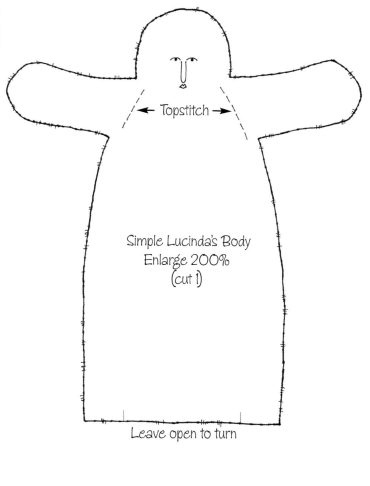

Topstitch

Simple Lucinda's Body
Enlarge 200%
(cut 1)

Leave open to turn

Topstitch

1. Placed fabric piece on the feed dogs, just under presser foot. Lower the presser foot and take two or three stitches forward, then reverse the machine two or three stitches to keep the thread from unraveling. This step is called backstitching. Finish stitching the area to be stitched, then backstitch at the end, to prevent unraveling. See Diagram A at right. Lift the presser foot up, and clip the threads.

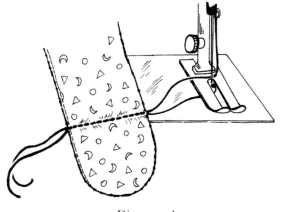

Diagram A

Lovey Dovey
(Variation of Simple Lucinda)

Using the same methods that were used for Simple Lucinda on pages 44–47, create Lovey Dovey. Make her a Gathered T-dress with 5¾" width, length 7", and 2"-wide sleeves. Refer to **Gathered T-dress** on page 36. Make an apron from 3¼" x 5¼" piece of desired fabric. Gather-stitch along top to 2¼". Adhere apron onto dress, approximately 1" below neck. Embellish top edge of apron with buttons.

Make a cone hat from paper and wind yarn around the base of hat. Adhere ends in place. Adhere hat to top of head.

How do I make a cloth doll with sculpted fingers?

Sculpting fingers is actually quite easy. Before the hands and arms are stuffed, lines are lightly drawn onto the hands with pencil. Stitch along the pencil lines to form the fingers. The trick is to use pipe cleaners instead of stuffing. A length of pipe cleaner is folded in half and inserted into each opening.

Ella Ree *(Photo on page 50)*

Here's how:

Creating the Doll

1. Using **Ella Ree's** patterns on page 52, prepare patterns. Refer to **Preparing the Patterns** on page 16.

2. Trace and stitch to create body, arms, and legs for doll. Refer to **Trace and Stitch**, Steps 2a–2b on pages 44 and 46. After tracing body, turn piece over and trace face onto the opposite side of fabric. *Note: The face will now be on the RIGHT side of the fabric.* Place piece face down, again.

3. Finish the **Trace and Stitch** process, Steps 2c-2d. Stuff head. Refer to **Stuffing the Doll Pieces** on page 20.

4. Sculpt fingers. Refer to **Sculpting the Fingers** on pages 16–17.

5. Attach legs. Refer to **Inserted Legs** on page 22.

6. Sculpt nose. Refer to **Sculpting the Nose** on pages 20–21.

Painting the Doll

1. Transfer face onto doll. Refer to **Sculpted Face Transfer** on page 24. Do not transfer dotted lines on pattern onto cloth.

2. Using stencil brush, dry-brush cheeks with red paint. Refer to **Cheeks** on page 29.

Continued on page 51.

2
technique

What you need to get started:

Materials & Tools:

- General Items on page 12
- Painting Items on page 13
- Sewing Items on page 14
- Acrylic paints: black; red
- Black fine-tipped permanent marker
- Button
- Coordinating embroidery floss
- Cotton print scraps for legs and bloomers
- Felts: for dress, 2" x 22"; scraps for decorations, collar, hat, shoes, skirt, sleeves
- Matte spray sealer
- Paintbrushes: liner; tiny stencil
- Pipe cleaners
- Polyester stuffing
- Tea-dyed muslin scraps for arms and body
- Yarns for hair and sleeve/ skirt edging

Continued from page 49.

3. Using stylus, paint lips with red paint. Refer to **Simple Lips** on page 31.

4. Using marker, paint eyes on doll. Refer to **Simple Eyes** on page 30.

Dressing the Doll

1. Using **Ella Ree's Shoe** pattern, trace and stitch shoes on felt. Trim seam allowance on shoe to a scant ⅛". Place shoes on feet.

2. Hand-stitch shoelaces with embroidery floss. Insert needle into upper-right dot as shown on pattern, exiting from upper-left dot. Leave a 4" tail. Cross over to lower-right dot, and exit from lower-left dot. Reinsert needle into lower-right dot, exiting from upper-left dot. See **Diagram A** above. Cut a 4" tail.

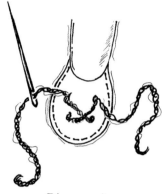

Diagram A

3. Tie a bow with tails. Place a dot of glue in center to secure. Trim tails.

4. Cut two 8"-square pieces from desired fabric. Make bloomers with a 5" inseam. Refer to **Bloomers** on page 34. See **Gather Stitch** on page 60.

5. Cut 8" x 20" piece from felt. Make skirt. Refer to **Skirts** on pages 36–37, gathering it just under arms.

6. Adhere yarn onto lower edge of skirt, overlapping ends in back. Cut ends and adhere into place.

7. Using **Ella Ree's Sleeve** pattern, cut out from felt. Adhere yarn around sleeve edges, overlapping ends. Cut ends and adhere into place. Hand-stitch arms onto shoulders.

8. Using **Ella Ree's Collar** pattern, cut out collar from felt. Using embroidery needle, buttonhole-stitch collar with embroidery floss to embellish. See **Buttonhole Stitch** on page 52. Adhere top corners of collar onto doll.

Ella Ree's Back View

9. Cut two 1" x 1½" hearts from felt. Cut two ¾" x 1" hearts from felt.

10. Cut five 1¼" circles from felt. Cut five ¾" squares from felt.

11. Center and whipstitch a smaller heart on top of a larger heart. Repeat for remaining hearts. See Whipstitch on page 60.

12. Whipstitch one set of hearts onto lower part of sleeve. Repeat on other sleeve.

13. Center and whipstitch one square onto one circle. Repeat for remaining shapes. Center and stitch one button onto each square with one strand of floss.

14. Whipstitch completed shapes ½" up from skirt bottom evenly around skirt edge.

15. Using fabric marker and starting at back seam of dress, draw a continuous loop design around all five shapes, ending at back seam of dress.

16. Trace loop design with glue. Place yarn on glue to adhere. Trim excess yarn at back seam.

17. Cut 3½" circle from felt for hat. Cut 1" circle out of hat.

Creating a Hairdo

1. Using yarn, create hairdo. Refer to **Embroidery Floss, Thread & Yarn** on page 33.

2. Pull hat over head. Wrap a torn strip of fabric around crown of head, covering center hole. Tie at the back with 2" tails. Adhere hat in several places to secure.

Buttonhole Stitch

1. Bring needle up at A; go down at B. Come up again at C, keeping thread under needle. Go down at D.

2. Repeat, making all stitches equal in size.

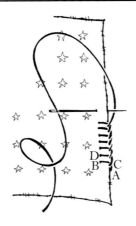

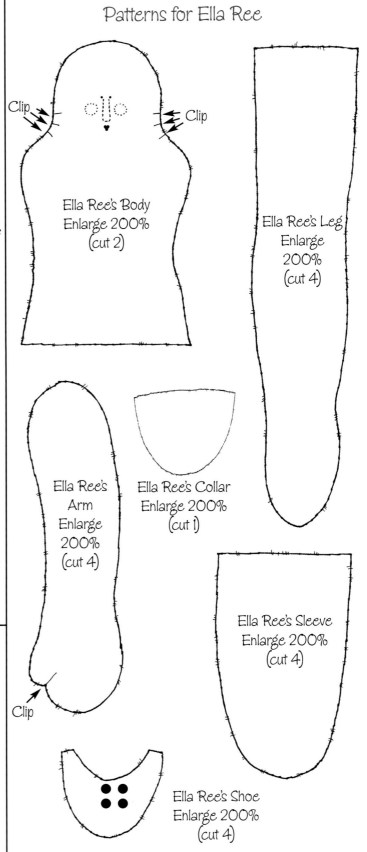

Patterns for Ella Ree

Clip

Ella Ree's Body
Enlarge 200%
(cut 2)

Clip

Ella Ree's Leg
Enlarge
200%
(cut 4)

Ella Ree's
Arm
Enlarge
200%
(cut 4)

Clip

Ella Ree's Collar
Enlarge 200%
(cut 1)

Ella Ree's Sleeve
Enlarge 200%
(cut 4)

Ella Ree's Shoe
Enlarge 200%
(cut 4)

How do I use patterns with seam allowances to create a doll?

This doll is created using patterns with seam allowances. Each pattern piece is pinned onto doubled fabric with right sides together, cut out, stitched together, and turned right side out. The body pieces are then assembled together. Many of this doll's clothes are made from patterns with seam allowances, such as the cap, the chemise, and the short gown.

Shaker Doll *(Photo on page 54)*

Here's how:

Creating the Doll

1. Using **Shaker Doll's** patterns on pages 58–60, prepare pattern pieces. Refer to **Preparing the Patterns** on page 16.

2. Use patterns to create doll. To use pattern pieces with seam allowances, use the following technique for each pattern piece.

a. Pin pattern onto a doubled piece of fabric with right sides together. Using fabric scissors, cut fabric along outer lines.

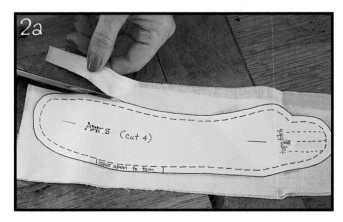

Continued on page 55.

What you need to get started:

Materials & Tools
- General Items on page 12
- Painting Items on page 13
- Sewing Items on page 14
- Acrylic paints: black; blue; dark brown; honey brown; dark burgundy; flesh; mauve; terra-cotta; white
- Blue/white checkered fabric for apron (⅓ yd)
- Blue/white striped ticking for short gown
- Brown gel-based stain
- Brown woven plaid for scarf (⅛ yd)
- Crackle medium
- Cream buttons (3)
- Cream felt for collar and cap (2 squares)
- Dark blue fabric for petticoat (½ yd)
- Embroidery floss: lt. brown; cream
- Fabric for bloomers and chemise (¼ yd)
- Gray curly wool roving for hair
- Matte spray sealer
- Muslin for body (½ yd)
- Paintbrushes: flat; liner; round stencil
- Pipe cleaners
- Polyester stuffing

53

Continued from page 53.

b. Stitch fabric together, following stitch lines indicated on pattern. Unless otherwise indicated, all patterns in this book have a ¼" seam allowance.

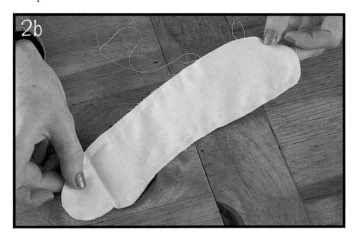

c. Turn stitched piece right side out.

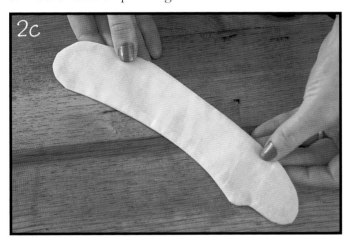

3. With right sides together, stitch **Head Back** pieces together on center back seam, leaving an opening as indicated on pattern. Press seam allowances open.

4. With right sides together, stitch **Head Front** to **Head Back**. Trim seam allowance to ⅛".

5. Turn head right side out. Stuff head firmly. Refer to **Stuffing the Doll Pieces** on page 20.

6. Sculpt nose. Refer to **Sculpting the Nose** on pages 20–21.

7. With right sides together, stitch torso, leaving an opening as indicated on pattern. Clip curves, turn right side out. Stuff torso firmly.

8. Pin head to neck. Hand-stitch head to neck with quilting thread.

9. With right sides together, stitch arms and legs, leaving an opening as indicated on pattern. Clip curves, turn right side out.

10. Sculpt fingers. Refer to **Sculpting the Fingers** on pages 16–17.

11. Attach arms. Refer to **Attaching the Arms** on page 22.

12. Attach legs. Refer to **Attaching the Legs** on pages 22–23.

Painting the Doll

1. Using flat brushes, base-coat arms approximately up to elbows, face, and neck of doll with flesh paint. Paint sock area up to knee with honey brown paint. Paint shoes with blue. Let paint dry. Sand lightly. Add a second coat of each color.

2. Transfer faces onto doll. Refer to **Sculpted Face Transfer** on page 24. Do not transfer dotted lines on pattern onto face.

3. Using stencil brush, dry-brush cheeks with terracotta paint. Refer to **Cheeks** on page 29.

4. Using liner brush, paint white areas of eye and highlights with white paint. Paint iris with dark brown paint. Paint eyebrows and line below eye with dark brown paint thinned with water. Refer to **Detailed Eyes** on pages 30–31.

5. Mix 1:1 ratio of mauve and white paints. Paint eyelid.

6. Using liner, paint pupil with black paint. Paint upper lid line with black paint thinned with water.

7. Paint inner lip line, and short line just below lip with dark brown paint. Refer to **Detailed Lips** on page 31.

8. Using liner brush, paint lips with dark burgundy paint thinned with water.

9. Mix 1:1 ratio of black and white paints. Dry-brush area between eyebrow and upper lid.

10. Antique doll. Refer to **Gel-based Stain** on page 29.

11. Apply crackle medium to arms (to elbows), face, and neck of doll. Refer to **Crackle Medium** on page 29.

Creating a Hairdo

1. Make hair by removing strings from curly wool roving. Using an iron, steam curls to slightly to straighten.

2. Pull roving into three 16" strands. *Note: Pull gently, and the wool will pull apart.* Place roving on a 2" square of muslin, centering strands, one next to the other.

3. Stitch muslin next to folded edge. Trim muslin into a football shape, with pointed ends at beginning and end of stitching.

4. Unfold roving, place on head, with seam down center of head. Position and adhere onto head.

5. Bring raw ends to nape of neck and twist loosely.

6. Fold under raw ends and adhere twisted hair onto back of head to cover bare spot.

Dressing the Doll

1. Using **Shaker Doll's Cap Side**, **Cap Back**, and **Cap Tie** patterns, place patterns on cream felt. Cut out. Pin side piece to back, as indicated on pattern. Stitch cap back to cap side piece. Trim seam allowance.

2. Center lower edge of cap back and side on cap tie. Pin in place. Overlap right side of lower edge of cap by ⅜₁₆".

Shaker Doll's Back View

3. Stitch close to edge of tie. See **Diagram A** below.

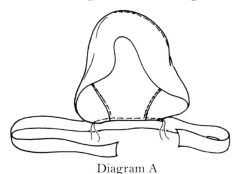

Diagram A

4. Using embroidery needle, buttonhole-stitch around the front edge of cap with cream floss. Refer to **Buttonhole Stitch** on page 52. *Note: Front edge may be folded back, if you like, or left like a sugar-scoop bonnet. Tie in a bow below chin.*

5. Cut 9½" x 10" piece from fabric. Make bloomers with a 5¼" inseam. Refer to **Bloomers** on page 34. See Gather Stitch on page 60.

6. Using **Chemise** pattern, cut chemise from desired fabric. With right sides together, stitch side seams. See **Diagram B** below.

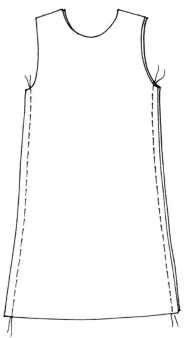

Diagram B

7. Press the seam allowances open and press under ¼" along all the top edges. Stitch in place. See **Diagram C** below.

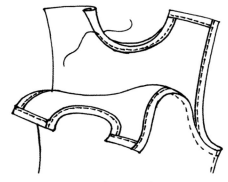

Diagram C

8. Press top and bottom raw edges under ¼" and hem.

9. Place on doll. Overlap shoulder tabs, and hand-stitch a button through both layers to secure. See **Diagram D** below.

Diagram D

10. Cut 15" x 17" piece from striped fabric. Fold fabric in half right sides together, then into quarters. Place **Short Gown** pattern on striped ticking, matching folded edges and cut out fabric. Stitch underarm seams. Clip corners, and turn right side out. Press seam allowances open, press under ¼" for sleeve hem, and ½" for skirt hem.

11. Stitch along hem lines.

12. Using embroidery needle, gather-stitch along waistline with cream floss, starting and stopping at center front of gown.

13. Place gown on doll. Pull stitches taut at waist and knot.

14. Using **Collar** pattern, place pattern on a folded piece of cream felt and cut out.

15. Using embroidery needle, buttonhole-stitch to finish outer edge with cream floss. Stitch a button on one of top corners, place around neck, and overlap in back. Adhere in place.

16. Tear 11" square from woven plaid. Make scarf by pulling a few threads to fringe edges about ¼".

17. Using embroidery needle, gather-stitch ¼" from edge with light brown floss.

18. Press scarf in half, diagonally, and place around shoulders. Tack in place.

19. Cut 14" x 30" piece from dark blue fabric. Make a petticoat. Refer to **Skirts** on pages 36–37.

20. Press under 1" hem and stitch hem with cream floss.

21. Tear 11" x 12" piece from checkered fabric. Gather-stitch along one short edge. Center on front of petticoat. Pull taut to fit and tack in place.

22. Gather-stitch along upper edge of petticoat, with apron, and place on doll. Pull gathers taut and knot. *Note: The short gown will hang over the top of the raw edges to hide them.*

Stitches

Whipstitch

1. Insert needle up through both layers of fabric at A. Draw thread out.

2. Go down at B and up at C in one motion, catching two or three threads.

3. Draw thread out gently. Repeat, covering entire area to secure fabric from unraveling.

Gather Stitch

1. Insert needle up through fabric at A, using one strand of thread.

2. Go down at B, creating a line of long straight stitches.

3. Come up at C, leaving an unstitched area between each stitch. Repeat for necessary length.

4. Pull the stitch and gather to desired tightness.

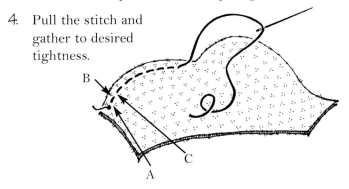

Patterns for Shaker Doll

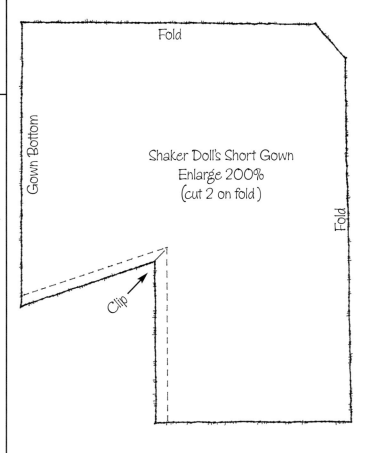

Fold

Gown Bottom

Fold

Shaker Doll's Short Gown
Enlarge 200%
(cut 2 on fold)

Clip

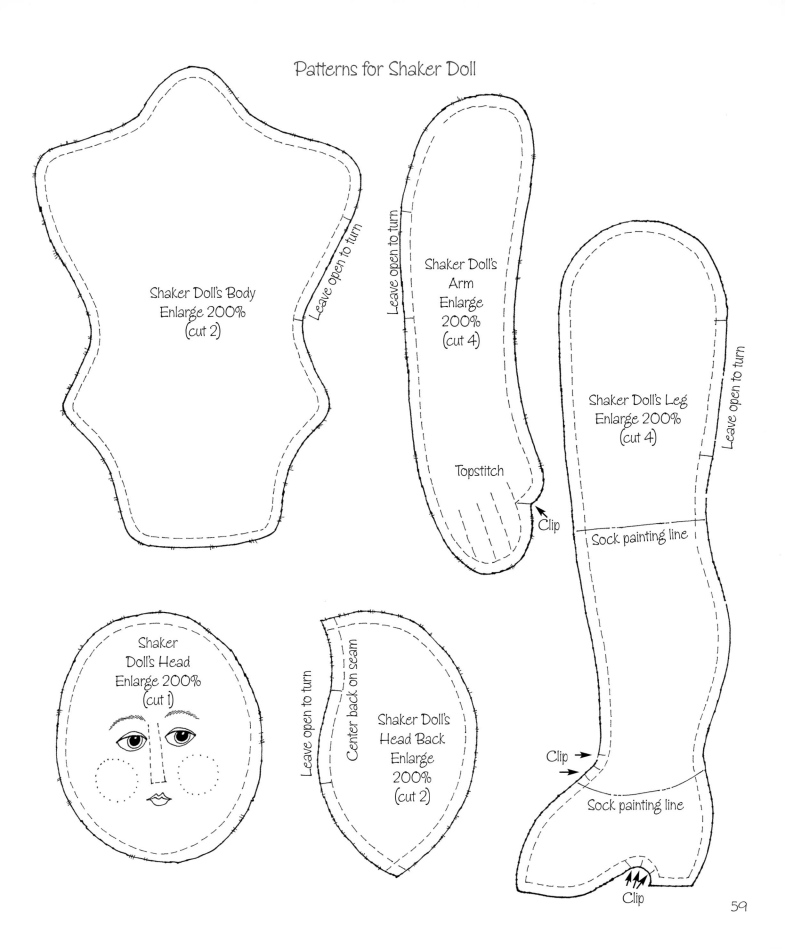

Patterns for Shaker Doll

Shaker Doll's Body
Enlarge 200%
(cut 2)

Leave open to turn

Leave open to turn

Shaker Doll's
Arm
Enlarge
200%
(cut 4)

Topstitch

Clip

Shaker Doll's Leg
Enlarge 200%
(cut 4)

Leave open to turn

Sock painting line

Shaker
Doll's Head
Enlarge 200%
(cut 1)

Leave open to turn

Center back on seam

Shaker Doll's
Head Back
Enlarge
200%
(cut 2)

Clip

Sock painting line

Clip

Patterns for Shaker Doll

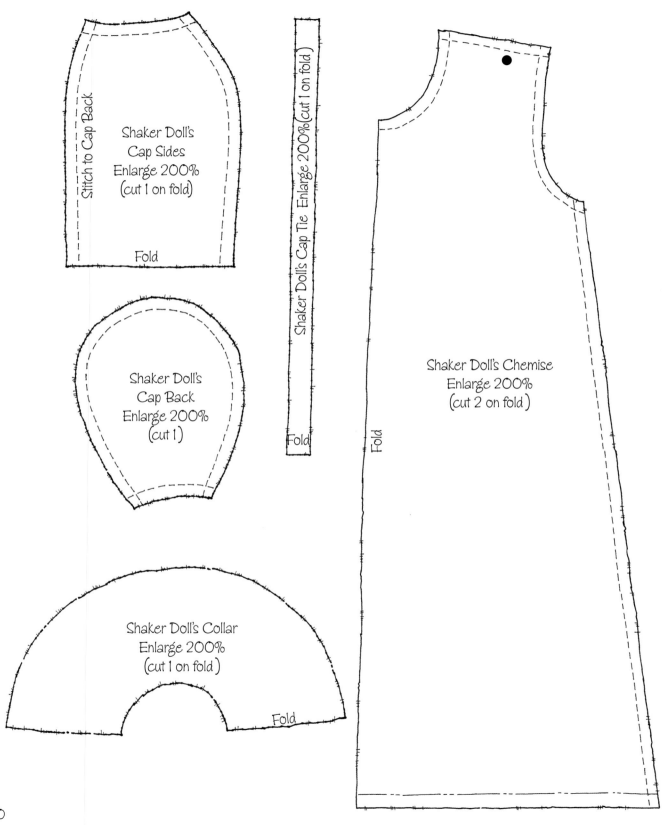

Stitch to Cap Back

Shaker Doll's
Cap Sides
Enlarge 200%
(cut 1 on fold)

Fold

Shaker Doll's Cap Tie Enlarge 200% (cut 1 on fold)

Fold

Shaker Doll's
Cap Back
Enlarge 200%
(cut 1)

Shaker Doll's Chemise
Enlarge 200%
(cut 2 on fold)

Fold

Shaker Doll's Collar
Enlarge 200%
(cut 1 on fold)

Fold

Moonlight Doll
(Variation of Shaker Doll)

Using the same patterns and methods that were used for Shaker Doll on pages 53–60, create Moonlight Doll. Her torso is made from blue fabric, so you do not have to make a separate piece of clothing. Her face and arms are base-coated with light yellow paint, then a wash of raw sienna applied. Moonlight's hair is made from long loops of blue yarn that are adhered to the top of her head.

Her top skirt is made from 9" x 45" piece of fabric. Her bottom skirt is made from a 12½" x 45" piece of fabric. Both skirts are finished by sewing a 1" strip of contrasting fabric, right sides together, then pressing the strip under so a fraction of an inch shows at lower edge of skirts. The strip is then hand-stitched in place. A collar is made from 6½" x 5½" piece of felt and embroidered. Her shoes are made with a pointed toe. Refer to **Making the Shoes** on pages 40–41.

4

technique

What you need to get started:

Materials & Tools
- General Items on page 12
- Painting Items on page 13
- Sewing Items on page 14
- Black fine-tipped permanent marker
- Button
- Cotton print fabrics: for apron (⅛ yd); for bloomers (¼ yd); for skirt and sleeves (½ yd); for wings (⅛ yd)
- Decorative paper scraps (3)
- Paintbrushes: liner; round stencil
- Red acrylic paint
- Red metallic yarn
- Tea-dyed muslin scrap for face
- Thin cotton batting scrap
- Wooden hearts, 4" tall (2)
- Wooden jumbo-sized craft sticks, ¾" x 6" (6)
- Wooden oval, 4" x 3"
- Wooden toothpicks (3)

How do I mix wooden and cloth elements to create a doll?

A doll can be created by combining wooden and cloth elements. For example on this project, the wooden oval was padded with batting and covered with muslin for the head. The wings, arms, legs, and body are all wooden, but embellished with various fabrics.

Miss Gardener

Here's how:
Creating the Doll

1. Using **Miss Gardener's Face** and **Spike** patterns on page 65, prepare pattern pieces. Refer to **Preparing the Patterns** on page 16.

2. Transfer facial features onto fabric. Refer to **Flat Face Transfer**, Steps 1–2 on page 24. Transfer outline of oval, adding ¾" for a cutting line.

3. Using fabric scissors, cut 4" x 3" piece from batting. Trim to fit oval. Place batting on top of wooden oval.

4. Gather-stitch along edge of muslin face. Place over padded oval. Pull threads taut and knot. Refer to **Gather Stitch** on page 60.

5. Using **Spike** patterns, make three spikes by folding paper along dotted lines as indicated on pattern, overlapping in back.

6. Adhere a piece of toothpick, with a little craft glue, in center of each paper spike to keep them from bending.

7. Adhere spikes onto back of head.

Continued on page 64.

Continued from page 62.

8. Adhere a craft stick onto lower back of head for a neck and body, overlapping head 2". See **Diagram A** below.

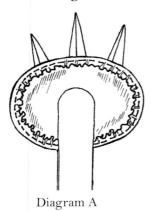

Diagram A

9. Tear 7" x 15" rectangle from print fabric for sleeves.

10. Fold one-third of top edge of the fabric toward center.

11. Using a small amount of glue, adhere one craft stick at each end. See **Diagram B** at right. *Note: The open edge of each 'sleeve' should be about 2¼" wide.*

Diagram B

Author's Tips:
• Eliminate the fabric on the face and paint the wooden base as shown on the Americana Angel doll on page 101.
• Experiment with different types of hair for her. How about painted wooden buttons?

12. Wrap yarn around center of sleeve tube. Tie a knot. See **Diagram C** below.

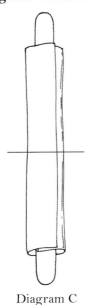

Diagram C

13. Adhere knotted area onto vertical craft stick, on lower part of back of head, a scant 1" up from chin level.

Painting the Doll

1. Using stencil brush, dry-brush cheeks with red paint. Refer to **Cheeks** on page 29.

2. Using marker, trace eyes and nose.

3. Using liner brush, paint mouth with red paint.

Dressing the Doll

1. Using fabric scissors, cut 7" x 28" piece from print fabric. Make bloomers just as you did the sleeves. Refer to Steps 10–12 on page 64 and above. *Note: The craft sticks overhang the edges by 1¼".*

2. Adhere onto body at lower edge of craft stick body piece.

3. Tear 15" x 22" piece from print fabric. Make skirt. Refer to **Skirts** on pages 36–37. Gather-stitch along top edge around neck, just below chin, under arms. Overlap in back and adhere in place.

4. Cut 11¾" x 22" piece from print fabric. Gather-stitch along one short edge. Wrap around neck, over top of skirt gathers.

Miss Gardener's Back View

5. Tie yarn fibers around neck. Knot.

6. Adhere a button over knot.

7. Cover hearts with print fabric for wings. Refer to **Covering the Wood with Decorative Paper** on pages 25–26. Adhere fabric onto wooden heart shapes, right sides up.

8. Adhere hearts onto back of doll about ¾" below lower edge of head for wings. Center and adhere another craft stick horizontally across wings to stabilize them. See **Diagram D** below. *Note: This can be used to hang the doll on a door hook.*

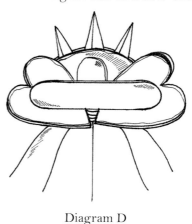

Diagram D

Patterns for Miss Gardener

Miss Gardener's Face

Enlarge 200%

Spike

Enlarge 200%
(cut 3)

technique

What you need to get started:

Materials & Tools

- General Items on page 12
- Painting Items on page 13
- Acrylic paints: black; medium brown; flesh; mauve; white
- Contrasting decorative papers (2)
- Paintbrushes: flat; liner; round stencil
- Rusty tin hearts (3)
- Silver craft wire
- Wood-toned spray stain
- Wooden buttons, ¾" (2)
- Wooden decorative plaque, 6" diameter
- Wooden hearts, 4" high (2)
- Wooden oval, 4" x 3"

How do I make a simple wooden doll?

This wooden doll is made using elements such as a wooden oval, wooden plaque, and wooden hearts. These elements are embellished and adhered together for this wooden angel. A hanger has been made from craft wire to display this doll as desired.

Simple Wooden Angel

Here's how:

Painting the Doll

1. Using **Simple Wooden Angel's Face** pattern on page 68, prepare pattern piece. Refer to **Preparing the Patterns** on page 16.

2. Prepare wood. Refer to **Preparing the Wood** on page 25. Using flat brush, base-coat oval with flesh paint for head.

3. Using stencil brush, dry-brush cheeks with mauve paint. Refer to **Cheeks** on page 29.

4. Transfer facial details onto wood. Refer to **Transferring Facial Features onto Wood** on page 26.

5. Paint nose line with medium brown paint.

6. Using stylus, dot eyes with black paint. Refer to **Simple Eyes** on page 30.

7. Using liner brush, paint tiny mouth with mauve paint.

Dressing the Doll

1. Adhere three tin hearts, upside down, onto back of head, so they extend from top like little spikes. Refer to **Nonfiber Items** on page 33.

Continued on page 68.

Continued from page 66.

2. Cover wooden hearts with papers for wings. Refer to **Covering the Wood with Decorative Paper** on pages 25–26.

3. Cover front of plaque with contrasting paper for body. Adhere head in place.

4. Paint buttons with white paint. Adhere buttons onto front of body.

Making a Hanger

1. Make a hanger, using the following technique:

a. Drill holes into plaque, following individual project instructions. For Simple Wooden Angel, see **Diagram A** below.

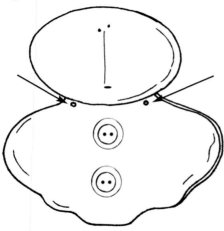

Diagram A

b. Using wire cutters, cut desired length from wire. *Note: The wire length depends on the length of hanger desired.*

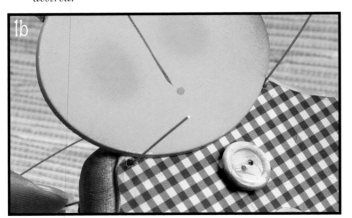

c. Insert wire from back of doll to front, making an arc at back of doll.

d. Using pencil, curl ends of wire.

Finishing the Doll

1. Adhere wings onto back of plaque.

2. Spray sides and back with wood-toned stain.

Author's Tip:
• Look for wonderful embellishments in the scrapbook section of the craft store. There are some amazing and fun items that can be used in dollmaking.

Pattern for Simple Wooden Angel

Simple Wooden Angel's Face

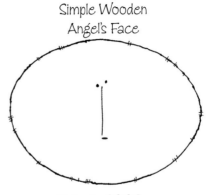

Enlarge 200%

Native American Angel

(Variation of Simple Wooden Doll)

Using the same methods that were used on the Simple Wooden Angel on pages 66–68, create this Native American Angel. Make hair by wrapping black floss around three fingers 10 times. Tie in the center with a piece of copper thread. Adhere hair onto top of head. Adhere a feather at side of hair. Create a necklace by stringing beads onto floral wire that is long enough to cover and go beneath doll's chin. Insert wire ends into hanger holes, exiting from the back of the doll. Twist wire ends together and trim excess wire. Adhere small flag onto front of body.

What you need to get started:

Materials & Tools

- General Items on page 12
- Painting Items on page 13
- Acrylic paints: black; light cream; mauve; pink; yellow
- Black craft wire
- Brooch
- Dowels: ¾" x 36"; 1" x 36" (2)
- Duct tape
- Floral foam, 3" x 4" x 8" (5)
- Garden gloves
- Metal wood screws, 1¼"
- Moss
- Natural dried excelsior
- Paintbrushes: flat; liner; round stencil
- Plaster of paris
- Ribbon scraps for bonnet
- Silk flowers for bonnet
- Small bushel-type basket, 7½" diameter
- Tin bucket
- Tulle scraps for bonnet
- Used women's clothing
- Wooden round paddle, 6" diameter

How do I make a life-sized wooden doll?

Make this life-sized wooden doll, using a wooden paddle and dowels. The dowel is secured in a bucket filled with plaster of paris. The doll is then embellishment with clothing from the local goodwill store and natural dried excelsior grass for hair.

Scarecrow Annie

Here's how:

Painting the Doll

1. Using **Scarecrow Annie's Face** pattern on page 73, prepare pattern piece. Refer to **Preparing the Patterns** on page 16.

2. Prepare wood. Refer to **Preparing the Wood** on page 25. Base-coat paddle with light cream paint. Float edges with yellow paint. Refer to **Floating Method** on page 28.

3. Transfer facial details onto paddle. Refer to **Transferring Facial Features onto Wood** on page 26. Do not transfer the dotted lines on pattern onto wooden paddle.

4. Using flat brush, apply pink paint thinned with water to nose area. Let dry.

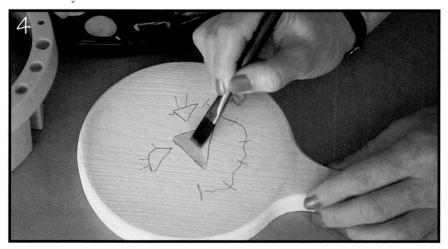

Continued on page 72.

Continued from page 70.

5. Using liner brush and mauve paint thinned with a water, cross-hatch nose.

6. Using liner brush and black paint thinned with water, outline nose.

7. Using stencil brush, dry-brush cheeks with mauve paint. Refer to **Cheeks** on page 29.

8. Using liner brush, outline eyes and nose with black paint thinned with water.

9. Paint eye highlights with yellow paint.

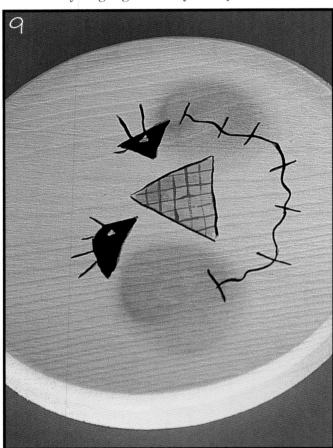

Assembling the Doll

1. Using duct tape, secure one large dowel to handle of paddle.

2. Drill two holes, one above the other, through handle and dowel. See **Diagram A** below.

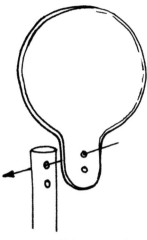

Diagram A

3. Adhere handle onto dowel, lining up the holes.

4. Using metal wood screws, secure handle to dowel.

5. Use same method to secure two dowels together, so dowels overlap about 18".

6. Place smaller dowel crosswise, just below chin area.

7. Drill holes into dowels. Secure with glue and craft wire.

8. Wrap craft wire around intersections several times, in an "X" shape. Pull taut before you twist.

9. Using wire cutters, trim excess wire away.

10. Mix plaster of paris, following manufacturer's instructions. Pour plaster of paris into bucket.

11. Insert bottom of dowel into bucket and secure stick figure so it will dry at proper angle. Let dry.

12. Finish filling bucket with floral foam. Cover with moss.

Dressing the Doll

1. Dress doll with clothing and garden gloves.

2. Tie scarves around neck.

3. Pin on brooch.

Creating a Hairdo

1. Adhere excelsior grass around top of head for hair.

2. Adhere basket onto top of head for bonnet.

3. Embellish bonnet with tulle, ribbons, and flowers.

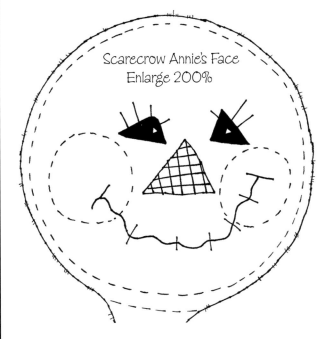

Pattern for Scarecrow Annie

Scarecrow Annie's Face
Enlarge 200%

Section 3: Beyond the Basics

1 project

What you need to get started:

Materials & Tools

- General Items on page 12
- Sewing Items on page 13
- Gold metallic thread
- Muslin, 7½" x 15" (3)
- Pearl fabric paint in bottle with pointed tip
- Polyester stuffing
- Satin ribbon roses
- Seed pearls

How do I make a cloth doll into an ornament?

Make a simple cloth doll into an ornament to hang on a Christmas tree or from a peg on a shelf. These dolls were made, using the Trace and Stitch technique. Pearl fabric paint, seed pearls, and satin roses embellish the angels. A hanger has been made from gold metallic thread.

Snow Angels

Here's how:

Creating the Dolls

1. Using **Snow Angel** patterns at right, prepare patterns. Refer to **Preparing the Patterns** on page 16.

2. Trace and stitch dolls. Refer to **Trace and Stitch**, Steps 2a–2d on pages 44–46.

3. Using pencil, lightly make decorative markings on each angel.

4. Stuff each angel. Refer to **Stuffing the Doll Pieces** on page 20. Stitch openings closed.

Dressing the Dolls

1. Hand-stitch seed pearls to lower edges of wings.

2. Apply fabric paint along markings. Let dry.

3. Adhere satin roses as desired.

4. Hand-stitch gold metallic thread to top of head for hanger.

Author's Tip:
• If you love to embroider, try couching lines with pearl cotton or cream silk ribbon to embroider angels before you cut and stitch the Snow Angels.

Patterns for Snow Angels

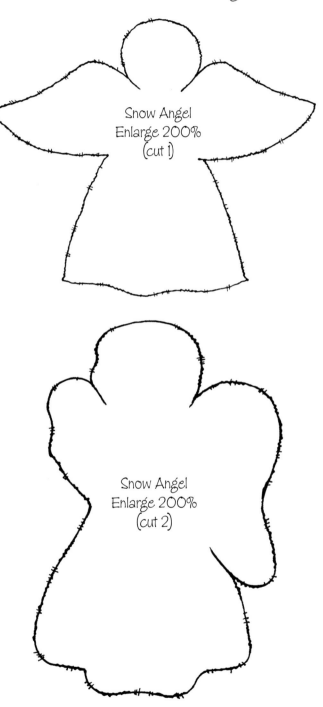

Snow Angel
Enlarge 200%
(cut 1)

Snow Angel
Enlarge 200%
(cut 2)

2 project

What you need to get started:

Materials & Tools
- General Items on page 12
- Painting Items on page 13
- Sewing Items on page 14
- Acrylic paints: black; light blue; brown; dark taupe brown; light flesh; raw sienna; medium tan; terra-cotta; white; wine; light yellow
- Contrasting fabric scraps for legs
- Coordinating embroidery floss
- Cotton prints, fat quarters (4) for clothing
- Curly wool roving scraps for hair
- Felt scraps for collar
- Matte spray sealer
- Oak-colored gel-based stain
- Paintbrushes: flat; liner; round stencil
- Pipe cleaners
- Polyester stuffing
- Twine
- Tea-dyed muslin, fat quarter for body
- Wooden clothespins
- Wooden craft embellishments (3)

How do I create a set of dolls?

Hanging three or more dolls by their fingertips from a clothesline is a cute way to display your dolls. These three cloth dolls were made using coordinating fabrics and many of the techniques used earlier in the book. Use decorative or antique clothespins for hanging. A collection of smaller dolls would also make a unique "valance" hanging from a curtain rod.

Clothesline Dolls

Here's how:
Creating the Dolls

1. Using **Clothesline Dolls'** patterns on page 81, prepare patterns. Refer to **Preparing the Patterns** on page 16.

2. Trace and stitch to create bodies, arms, and legs for three dolls. Refer to **Trace and Stitch**, Steps 2a–2b on pages 44 and 46. After tracing body, turn piece over.

3. Using stylus, transfer nose onto the opposite side of fabric. *Note: The face will now be on the RIGHT side of the fabric.* Place piece face down, again.

4. Finish the **Trace and Stitch** process, Steps 2c–2d. Stuff head. Refer to **Stuffing the Doll Pieces** on page 20.

5. Sculpt fingers. Refer to **Sculpting the Fingers** on pages 16–17.

6. Attach legs. Refer to **Inserted Legs** on page 22. Do not attach arms until later.

Continued on page 80.

Continued from page 78.

7. Sculpt nose. Refer to **Sculpting the Nose**, Steps 2–10 on pages 20–21.

Painting the Dolls

1. Using flat brush, base-coat face and arms with following colors: for Moonbeam, light yellow; for Blue Moon, light blue; for Mooning-for-You, light flesh.

2. Using **Clothesline Dolls' Body** pattern, transfer faces onto dolls. Refer to **Sculpted Face Transfer** on page 24.

3. Mix 1:1 ratio of raw sienna paint for a wash. Brush wash onto Moonbeam's head and hands. Blot with paper towel.

4. Using stencil brush, dry-brush cheeks for Moonbeam and for Mooning-for-You with terra-cotta paint. Dry-brush cheeks for Blue Moon with wine paint. Refer to **Cheeks** on page 29.

5. Using liner brush, paint irises with brown paint. Paint upper eye lids with medium tan paint. Paint pupils with black paint. Paint whites of eyes and highlights with white paint. Paint upper lid lines with black paint. Paint eyebrows and lower lid lines with dark taupe brown paint. Refer to **Detailed Eyes** on pages 30–31.

6. Paint inner lip line with brown paint. Paint lips with wine paint. Refer to **Detailed Lips** on page 31.

7. Antique Blue Moon's head and face with gel-based stain. Refer to **Gel-based stain** on page 29.

8. Spray with sealer.

Creating Hairdos

1. Unravel one 3"–4" length of curly wool roving for each doll. Adhere onto each head.

2. Braid a small section of roving on Mooning-for-You.

3. Make a little top knot on Moonbeam's head.

4. Tie 1"-wide strip of torn fabric around each doll's head and knot at front.

80

Mooning-for-You Close-up

5. Clip ends in an inverted "V" shape for Moonbeam. Repeat for Mooning-for-you.

Dressing the Dolls

1. Cut six 8"-square pieces from print fabric. Make bloomers with a 5" inseam for each doll. Refer to **Bloomers** on page 34.

2. Cut three 8" x 20" pieces from print fabrics. Make skirts. Refer to **Skirts** on pages 36–37. Pull taut just under arms.

3. Using **Clothesline Dolls' Sleeve** pattern, cut sleeves from print fabric. Make pillowcase sleeves. Refer to **Pillowcase Sleeves** on pages 38–39. Hand-stitch arms onto shoulders so they are pointing upward.

4. Using **Clothesline Dolls' Collar** pattern, trace and stitch collar from felt.

5. Using embroidery needle, buttonhole-stitch collar with embroidery floss to embellish. Refer to **Buttonhole-stitch** on page 52. Adhere top corners of collar onto doll.

6. Adhere wooden craft embellishments onto collar as desired.

7. Paint wooden clothespins as desired.

8. Using clothespins, pin dolls to a piece of twine.

Patterns for Clothesline Dolls

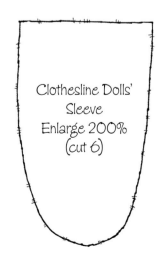

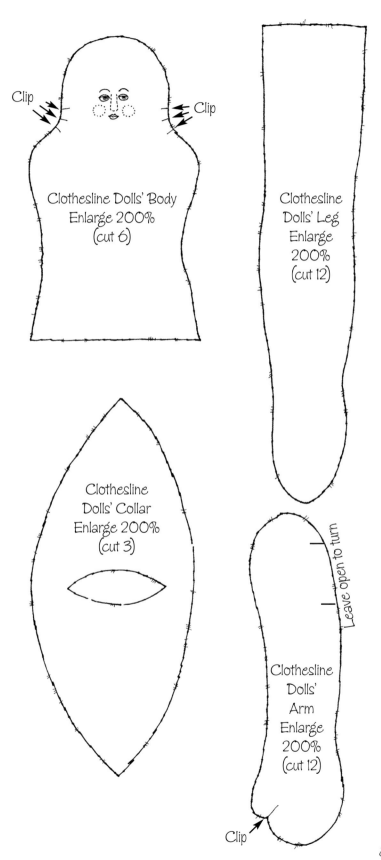

Blue Moon Close-up

Moon Beams Close-up

Miss Liberty
(Variation of Clothespin Doll)

Using the same methods that were used on the Ella Ree on pages 49–52 and the Clothesline Dolls on pages 78–82, create Miss Liberty and her clothes. Base-coat her skin with a baby-blue paint. After painting her facial features, antique her with stain. Refer to **Gel-based Stain** on page 29. Make Miss Liberty's hair by removing paper tube from green floss. Wind three metallic threads around floss lengthwise and stitch down the center. Adhere onto head. Make her a crown from gold felt and tack in place.

Use a needle to make a small hole in each of her hands. Cut 12" piece of wire. Insert wooden flag onto wire. Curl the wire randomly, then insert wire ends into hands from back to the front. Curl ends of wire to secure. Twist the garland onto wire.

3

project

What you need to get started:

Materials & Tools
- General Items on page 12
- Painting Items on page 13
- Sewing Items on page 14
- Black sewing thread
- Black wool roving for hair
- Bracelet for necklace
- Buttons (4)
- Dark rose pink acrylic paint
- Embroidery floss: black; light brown; dark brown
- Fabric for blanket (¼ yd)
- Flannel fabric for dress (½ yd)
- Gray suede scraps for moccasins
- Linen for body (½ yd)
- Polyester stuffing
- Red felt for belt
- Round stencil paintbrush

How do I make a doll with button-on joints?

Using button joints for arms and legs allow the limbs to swing more freely. This method is especially helpful when you want to pose your doll. The trick is using sturdy buttons and strong waxed thread. In this project, only the legs have joints, but the arms could be created in the same matter. The legs are both attached at the same time with the needle going through the button at the hip, through the body, through the other hip and button, and back again.

Native American

Here's how:

Creating the Doll

1. Using **Shaker Doll's** patterns for **Head Back**, **Arm**, and **Body** on page 59 and **Native American's** patterns on page 87, prepare patterns. Refer to **Preparing the Patterns** on page 16.

2. Create doll from linen, but leave fingers unstitched. Refer to **Shaker Doll**, Steps 2–5 on pages 53 and 55.

3. Stitch torso. Refer to **Shaker Doll**, Steps 7–9 and Step 11 on page 55.

4. Attach legs. Refer to **Button-on Joints** on page 23.

5. Using **Native American's Head** pattern, transfer face onto doll. Refer to **Flat Face Transfer** on page 24.

6. Using embroidery needle, french-knot eyes, with one strand of black embroidery floss, wrapping needle three times. See **French Knot** on page 87.

7. Stem-stitch nose, lips, and chin with single thread of dark brown floss. See **Stem Stitch** on page 87.

Continued on page 86.

Continued from page 84.

Painting the Doll

1. Using stencil brush, dry-brush cheeks with dark rose pink paint. Refer to **Cheeks** on page 29.

Creating a Hairdo

1. Stitch down center of roving with black thread. Adhere onto head. Refer to **Wool Roving** on page 32. Braid ends and tie with light brown floss.

Dressing the Doll

1. Cut two 17" x 17½" pieces from flannel fabric. Make T-dress with a 3"–4" slit for back neck opening. Refer to **T-dress** on pages 34–35.

2. Press under raw edges along T-dress neckline, sleeves, and lower hem. Using embroidery needle, whipstitch edges with dark brown embroidery floss. Refer to **Whipstitch** on page 60. Place on doll and hand-stitch back opening closed.

3. Tear 8" x 26" piece from blanket fabric. Press and drape over left shoulder.

4. Cut 28" x 1¾" strip from red felt for belt. Cut ends into 1½" fringes. Tie around waist, securing the "blanket."

5. Place bracelet around neck.

6. Make moccasins. Refer to **Making the Shoes** on pages 40–41.

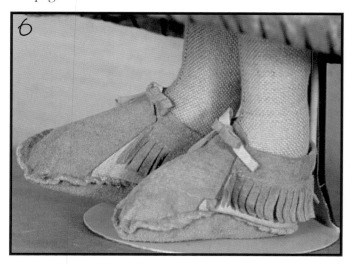

Native American's Back View

Patterns for Native American

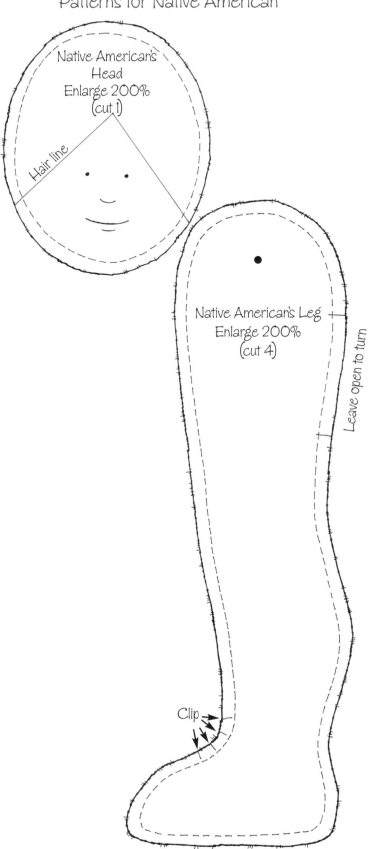

Native American's
Head
Enlarge 200%
(cut 1)

Hair line

Native American's Leg
Enlarge 200%
(cut 4)

Leave open to turn

Clip

Stitches

French Knot

1. Thread a needle and make a knot in the end of the thread. Bring the needle up through the fabric at A and hold the thread, close to the fabric, with your left hand while you wrap the needle loosely with the thread, three times.

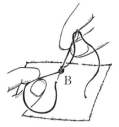

2. Insert the needle back into the fabric, just next to the exit point of the thread at B, and pull the thread until the loose thread pulls through the knot.

Stem Stitch

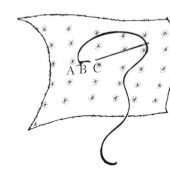

1. Bring needle up through fabric at C, go down at B. Come back up at C.

2. Go down at A, then back up at B.

3. Repeat, making a solid line of stitching.

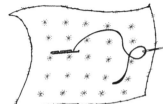

4
project

What you need to get started:

Materials & Tools
- General Items on page 12
- Painting Items on page 13
- Sewing Items on page 14
- Acrylic paints: black; gray-blue; brown; cream; flesh; terra-cotta; warm tan
- Black felt scraps for boots
- Contrasting embroidery floss
- Cotton prints: for hat (⅓ yd); for pants (⅓ yd); for shirt (fat quarter)
- Felted wool: red for coat 11" x 33"; brown scraps for trims
- Gray wool crepe for hair
- Matte spray sealer
- Muslin for body (½ yd)
- Oak-colored gel-based stain
- Paintbrushes: flat; liner; round stencil
- Pipe cleaners
- Polyester stuffing
- Wired-silk pine greenery
- Wooden moon/predrilled hole

How do I make a doll with a beard?

There are many types of fiber available that can be used for a beard, depending on the type of look you want to achieve. Soft and silky fibers give the doll a dressier feel, while the wool fiber used for Father Christmas gives a more primitive look. The easiest way to adhere the beard to the doll is to use craft glue.

Father Christmas

Here's how:
Creating the Doll

1. Using **Shaker Doll's** patterns for **Head Back** and **Arm** on page 59 and **Father Christmas's** patterns on page 93, prepare pattern pieces. Refer to **Preparing the Patterns** on page 16.

2. Create doll from muslin. Refer to **Shaker Doll**, Steps 2–12 on pages 53 and 55.

Painting the Doll

1. Using **Santa Head's** pattern, transfer face onto doll. Refer to **Sculpted Face Transfer** on page 24.

2. Using flat brush, base-coat face, neck, and arms with flesh paint. Sand lightly when dry.

3. Using stencil brush, dry-brush cheeks, end of nose, and lips with terra-cotta paint. Refer to **Cheeks** on page 29.

4. Using liner brush, paint iris area with gray-blue paint. Paint eyelid with warm tan paint. Paint pupil with black paint. Refer to **Detailed Eyes** on pages 30–31.

5. Paint white of eye with cream paint. Using stylus, apply a small highlight in pupil.

6. Using liner brush and black paint thinned with water, paint a very fine line at upper eyelid.

Continued on page 90.

Continued from page 88.

7. Paint a wrinkle underneath each eye with brown paint thinned with water.

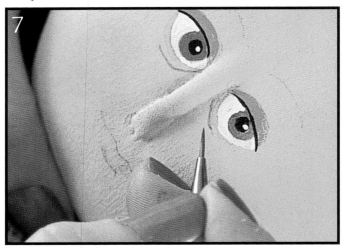

8. Paint inner lip line and line underneath lower lip with brown paint. Let dry.

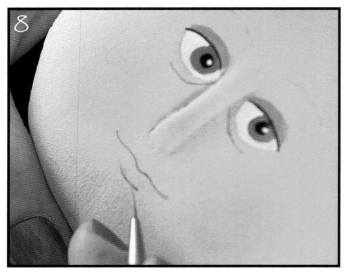

9. Using gel stain, antique doll. Refer to **Gel-stain** on page 29.

10. Spray with sealer.

Father Christmas's Back View

90

Dressing the Doll

1. Make shirt by folding fabric in half, then into quarters. Cut shirt using **Diagram A** below:

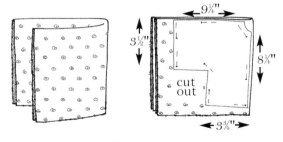

Diagram A

2. Unfold shirt with right sides together; stitch underarm seams. Clip corners and turn right side out. Press. See **Diagram B** at right.

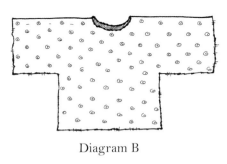

Diagram B

3. Cut 2" slit in center back of neckline. Press under ¼" along bottom edge of shirt.

4. Using embroidery needle, gather-stitch around bottom hem of shirt with embroidery floss. Refer to **Gather Stitch** on page 60.

5. Gather-stitch around sleeve openings. Place on doll and pull gathers taut. Knot.

6. Cut two 11" x 12" pieces from desired fabric. Make pants with a 7" inseam. Refer to **Bloomers** on page 34. *Note: The 11" edges are the sides of the pants.*

7. Gather-stitch around waist and lower pant leg openings. Place on doll and pull gathers taut. Knot.

8. Using **Boot** pattern, cut out boots from felt. Place two pieces together, stitching around back, bottom, and front to dot. Clip to dot.

9. Turn boots right side out and place on feet. Fold open ends of boots over each other to fit ankle.

10. Stitch three "X"s down front of boot opening with embroidery floss to keep it closed. Refer to **Ella Ree's** shoes, Steps 2–3 on page 51.

11. Pull pant leg up slightly so raw edges are at top of boot.

12. Cut thick felt cuffs for bottom of pants and bottom edges of sleeves. Leave enough room to overlap cuffs ¼". Adhere in place with craft glue, covering raw gathered edges.

13. Cut 16½" x 6" piece on fold. Stitch to fold. See **Diagram C** at right.

Diagram C

14. Trim seam allowance, then turn hat right side out and press. Insert a small amount of stuffing into pointed end of hat. Set hat aside.

Creating a Hairdo

Note: The wool fibers used in the following photos are wool roving. The wool fibers used on Father Christmas are wool crepe. Both wool fibers are applied in the same way, folding under the top edge and adhering in place.

1. Remove string from wool and pull strands apart every 4½" or 5". *Note: Pulling wool apart looks better than cutting it with scissors.*

2. Select a few strands for eyebrows. Cut them 1" or a little less. Twist fibers together, dampening your fingers a little with water as you work. Carefully adhere each twist over eyes for eyebrows.

3. Pull a few strands of wool for mustache. Trim piece to about 2". Twist strands in center and adhere twisted area just below nose.

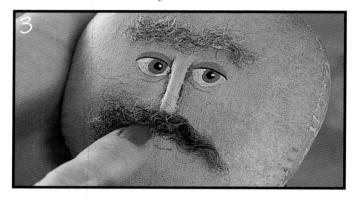

4. Use three pieces of wool for beard. Fold under top edge and adhere. Press in place.

5. Lay two pieces of wool across top of head, centering the fiber on the head. Do not fold ends under. Adhere onto top of head.

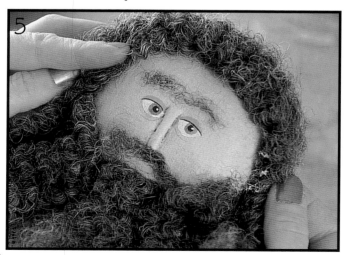

6. Lay three pieces of wool on back of head, folding under top end and adhere onto back of head.

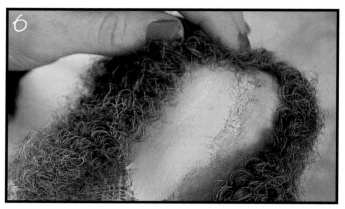

7. Place hat on head, just a little above eyebrows, covering back of head where there is no hair, and adhere.

8. Wrap felt trim around base of hat, overlapping ends ⅛". Cut and adhere trim to the hat, beginning and ending at back of head.

Finishing the doll

1. Fold 11" x 33" piece from thick felt in half so it is 16½" x 11" for coat.

2. Using **Coat Neck** pattern, place pattern on fold edge of coat and cut out neck shape from top center. Make a slit up center front of felt to neckline for coat. See **Diagram C** at right.

Diagram C

3. With wrong sides together, stitch sides together to within 5" of folded top edge.

4. Using embroidery needle, buttonhole-stitch side seams, then around edges of coat with embroidery floss. Refer to **Buttonhole Stitch** on page 52.

5. Using glue gun and glue sticks, adhere wired greenery in a swirl pattern. *Note: Approximately two-thirds of the front of each side is covered with the design.*

6. Hand-stitch a wooden moon to end of cap.

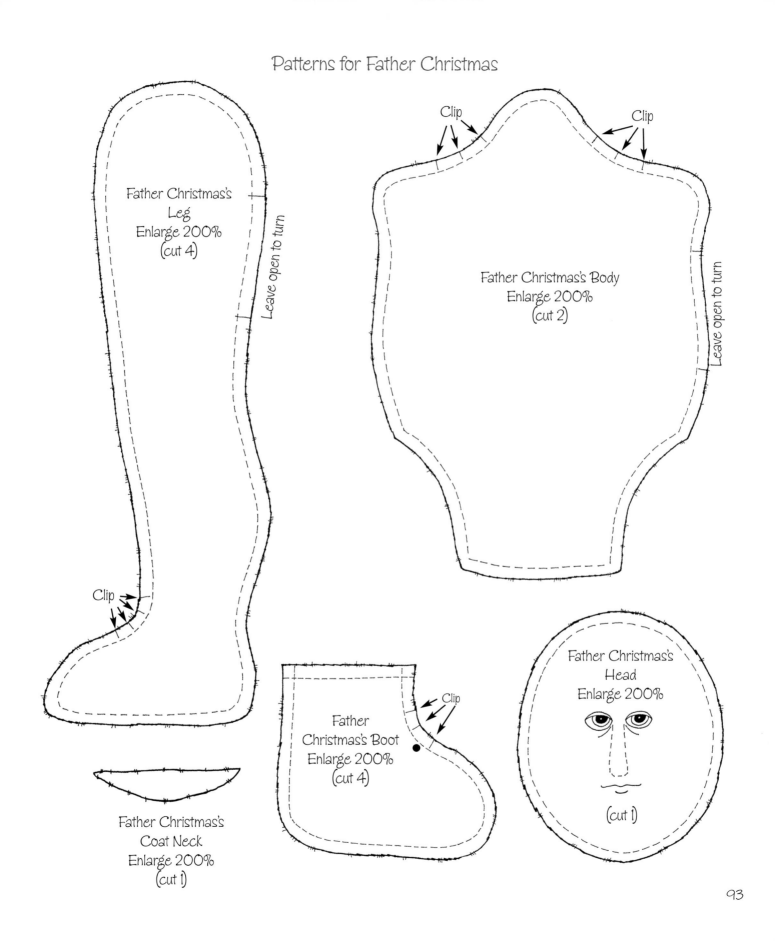

Patterns for Father Christmas

Father Christmas's
Leg
Enlarge 200%
(cut 4)

Leave open to turn

Clip

Father Christmas's
Coat Neck
Enlarge 200%
(cut 1)

Clip   Clip

Father Christmas's Body
Enlarge 200%
(cut 2)

Leave open to turn

Clip

Father
Christmas's Boot
Enlarge 200%
(cut 4)

Father Christmas's
Head
Enlarge 200%

(cut 1)

5
project

What you need to get started:

Materials & Tools

- General Items on page 12
- Painting Items on page 13
- Sewing Items on page 14
- Acrylic paints: black; dark brown; medium reddish-brown; burgundy; flesh; light tan; off-white
- Cotton fabrics: for bloomers (⅛ yd); for jacket (¼ yd); for skirt (¼ yd)
- Crackle medium
- Crocheted lace doily, 6½" diameter
- Flannel for legs (⅛ yd)
- Gold curly wool roving for hair
- Matte spray sealer
- Muslin for body and arms (¼ yd)
- Narrow ribbon scrap
- Oak-colored gel-based stain
- Paintbrushes: flat; liner; round stencil
- Panel of antique lace for skirt front
- Pipe cleaners
- Polyester stuffing
- Satin ribbon rose
- Trims

How do I make a doll with sculpted toes?

If you aren't planning to make shoes for your doll, sculpted toes are a delightful detail. Sculpting toes differs from sculpting fingers in that the toes are stuffed prior to the stitching. After the feet have been stuffed, the toe lines are marked lightly with a pencil and then hand-stitched to form chubby little toes.

Josephine

Here's how:
Creating the Doll

1. Using **Josephine's** patterns on pages 98, prepare patterns. Refer to **Preparing the Patterns** on page 16.

2. Create doll from muslin. With right sides together, stitch head to body before stitching the body together. See **Diagram A** at right. Refer to **Shaker Doll**, Steps 2–2c on pages 53 and 55 for body and arms for doll. Leave unstuffed until after legs are attached.

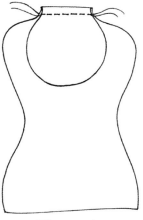

Diagram A

Continued on page 96.

Continued from page 94.

3. Sculpt toes. Referring to **Sculpting the Toes** on pages 17–19.

4. Sculpt nose. Refer to **Sculpting the Nose** on pages 20–21.

5. Sculpt fingers. Refer to **Sculpting the Fingers** on pages 16–17.

6. Stuff arms and set aside. Refer to **Stuffing the Doll Pieces** on page 20.

7. Attach legs. Refer to **Inserted Legs** on page 22.

Painting the Doll

1. Using flat brush, base-coat head and arms with flesh paint.

2. Using **Josephine's Head** pattern, transfer face onto doll. Refer to **Sculpted Face Transfer** on page 24.

3. Using stencil, dry-brush cheeks with burgundy paint. Refer to **Cheeks** on page 29.

4. Using liner brush, paint iris with medium reddish-brown paint. Paint eyelid with light tan paint. Paint lid line and eyebrow with dark brown paint. Paint pupil with black paint. Paint whites of eyes and highlights with off-white paint. Refer to **Detailed Eyes** on pages 30–31.

5. Paint inner lip line with dark. brown paint. Paint lips with burgundy. Refer to **Detailed Lips** on page 31.

6. Apply crackle medium onto face to create an aged look. Refer to **Crackle Medium** on page 29. Antique face. Refer to **Gel-based Stain** on page 29.

7. Spray with sealer.

Creating a Hairdo

1. Make hair. Refer to **Curling Wool Roving** on page 32.

Dressing the Doll

1. Cut 6½" x 10" piece from desired fabric. Make bloomers with a 7" inseam. Refer to **Bloomers** on page 34.

2. Cut 13" x 32" piece from desired fabric. Make skirt. Refer to **Skirts** on pages 36–37. Place bottom edges of skirt and lace with right sides together. Stitch.

3. Press seam allowances toward skirt. Gather-stitch antique lace to hemmed lower edge. Refer to **Gather Stitch** on page 60.

4. Cut two 13" x 7" pieces from fabric. Make jacket with 3½"-wide and 4"-deep sleeves. Refer to **Gathered T-dress** on page 36. See **Diagram A** at right.

Diagram A

5. Cut "A" shaped slit up front of jacket with bottom section of slit being 1" wide. Machine-hem all edges.

6. Make collar. Refer to **Lace Doily** on page 39. Adhere collar onto jacket.

7. Embellish collar with tiny bow. Adhere satin ribbon flower onto side of head.

Grace
(Variation of Josephine)

Using the same methods that were used on the Josephine on pages 94–98, create Grace. Her eyes are French knots, and her mouth is stitched twice with red thread. Antique her faces and hands with acrylic paint. Refer to **Acrylic Paint** on page 29. Make fancy sleeves and appliqué felt motifs onto her double skirts. Create Grace's hairdo by wrapping and adhering yarn around a stained spool. Center and hot-glue the spool onto her head.

Josephine's Back View

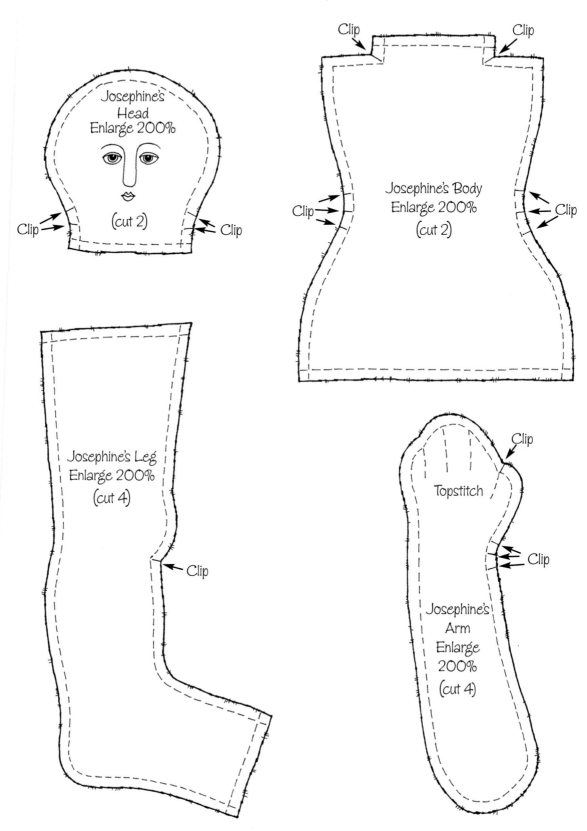

Patterns for Josephine

Josephine's
Head
Enlarge 200%

(cut 2)

Clip

Clip

Clip

Clip

Josephine's Body
Enlarge 200%
(cut 2)

Clip

Clip

Josephine's Leg
Enlarge 200%
(cut 4)

Clip

Clip

Topstitch

Clip

Josephine's
Arm
Enlarge
200%
(cut 4)

How do I make a doll from a clothespin?

A clothespin doll is made from a peg-style wooden clothespin. A simple face is added to the top and embroidery floss is used for the hairdo. Fabric and ribbon scraps are all that is needed to clothe this doll. The clothespin is adhered onto a wooden base for support. Clothespin dolls make ideal party favors, seasonal decorations, or place-card holders.

Miss Glory *(Photo on page 100)*

Here's how:
Creating the Doll

1. Using flat brush, paint top of clothespin with flesh paint for head. Paint bottom of clothespin with black paint for feet.

2. Using tiny stencil brush, dry-brush cheeks with mauve paint. Refer to **Cheeks** on page 29.

3. Using stylus, make mouth with mauve paint. Refer to **Simple Lips** on page 31.

4. Make eyes with black paint. Refer to **Simple Eyes** on page 30.

Creating a Hairdo

1. Make hair by wrapping embroidery floss around two fingers 10 times or less. Tie in center with a piece of embroidery floss.

2. Adhere hair onto top of head. Trim to 1" wide. Fluff hair.

Dressing the Doll

1. Tear 2¾" x 6½" piece from fabric. Match and stitch along 6½" edges for back seam. Press seam allowances open. Turn right side out and fray bottom edges for skirt. Gather-stitch along top edge and place on doll. Pull gather taut and knot. Refer to **Gather Stitch** on page 60.

6
project

What you need to get started:

Materials & Tools
- General Items on page 12
- Painting Items on page 13
- Sewing Items on page 14
- Acrylic paints: black; flesh; mauve
- Fabric scraps for skirt and sleeves
- Flesh-colored paper
- Orange embroidery floss
- Paintbrushes: flat; tiny round stencil
- Peg-style wooden clothespin
- Ribbon scraps for scarf
- Wooden shape for base

Miss Tahiti
(Variation of Miss Glory)

99

2. Tear 2" x 1½" piece from desired fabric. Make sleeves by stitching short edges together. Fray bottom edge of sleeve, gather-stitch along top edge of sleeve and place on doll. Adhere onto shoulder.

3. Using craft scissors, cut a hand the size of a pencil eraser from paper. Adhere hand into sleeve.

4. Tie ribbon around neck.

Finishing the Doll

1. Adhere paper onto wooden shape for a base. Refer to **Covering Wood with Decorative Paper** on doll on pages 25–26.

2. Adhere doll onto base.

How do I make a doll from a wooden paddle?

This paddle doll was made from an ordinary, unpainted wooden paddle. You will be surprised at the results you can get from a few pieces of wood, some scrapbook paper, paint, and imagination.

Americana Angel *(Photo on page 102)*

Here's how:

Creating the Doll

1. Using **Americana Angel's Face** pattern on page 103, prepare pattern piece. Refer to **Preparing the Patterns** on page 16.

2. Prepare wood. Refer to **Preparing the Wood** on page 25. Using flat brush, base-coat wooden oval (face) and craft sticks (hands) with flesh paint.

3. Base-coat top fourth of face with taupe-brown paint for hair area. Let dry. Lightly sand face and hands.

4. Using stencil brush, dry-brush cheeks with dark flesh paint. Refer to **Cheeks** on page 29. Using stylus, dot each cheek with light cream paint.

5. Paint button with gray-blue paint.

6. Using **American Angel's Face** pattern, transfer eyes, nose, and mouth onto wood. Refer to **Transferring Facial Features onto Wood** on page 26. Do not transfer dotted lines on pattern onto wooden paddle.

7. Using liner brush, paint facial details with black paint.

8. Spray face and hands with sealer.

Creating a Hairdo

1. Wrap ribbon around head. Tie a square knot and trim ends.

2. Make hair by wrapping yarn around four fingers, seven times. Tie in center with a piece of yarn. Repeat two times, creating three hair bundles.

7

project

What you need to get started:

Materials & Tools

- General Items on page 12
- Painting Items on page 13
- Acrylic paints: black; gray-blue; taupe-brown; flesh; dark flesh; light cream
- Black craft wire
- Checkered ribbon, 1½" wide (⅛ yd) for hair bow
- Curly yarn fiber for hair
- Decorative papers (6)
- Flag, 5½" x 4"
- Glossy wood-toned spray stain
- Matte spray sealer
- Paintbrushes: flat; liner; round stencil
- Rusty star, 3"
- Scallop-edged scissors
- Twine
- Wooden button, ¾"
- Wooden hearts, 4" tall (2)
- Wooden jumbo-sized craft sticks, ¾" x 6" (2)
- Wooden oval shape, 4" x 3"
- Wooden paddle, 18½" x 4½"

3. Adhere onto top of head, so it cascades over scarf a little. Using fabric scissors, clip loops.

Dressing the Doll

1. Cover craft sticks with paper, leaving 2" at one end of each uncovered, for the hands. Refer to **Covering the Wood with Decorative Paper** on pages 25–26.

2. Cut two ⅜" x ¼" strips from paper. Adhere onto sleeve for cuffs.

3. Cover hearts with paper. Cover paddle handle with paper to simulate feet.

4. Cut 4¼" x 5½" piece from desired paper for lower skirt. Adhere onto paddle.

5. Cut 4¼" x 11" piece from desired paper for upper skirt. Using scallop-edged scissors, trim one end of paper.

6. Adhere star and button onto lower skirt as shown in photo on page 102.

7. Adhere head at upper-left corner, at a slight angle. Adhere wings ¾" from head.

8. Adhere one arm onto front of doll at side of chin, so it extends 2½" from bottom of doll. Adhere remaining arm horizontally onto paddle ¼" above lowest point of chin.

Making a Hanger

1. Drill a hole through upper-left hand corner between wings and chin for hanging. Drill another hole 1½" from upper-right corner.

2. Make a hanger. Refer to **Making a Hanger**, Steps 1b–1d on page 68.

Finishing the Doll

1. Adhere flag onto horizontal arm, so the flag is floating above head. Tie a piece of twine around hand and flag stick to secure.

2. Spray sides and back of doll, as well as flag, with wood-toned stain.

Pattern for Americana Angel

Americana Angel's Face Enlarge 200%

Pumpkin Woman

(Variation of Americana Angel)

Using the same methods that were used for Americana Angel on pages 100–102 and above, create Pumpkin Woman. Use a 14" x 6½" wooden paddle and a round shape for her head. Her wood head is painted with a burnt-orange paint, with a little bit of terra-cotta dry-brushed for highlights. Her hair is a piece of twine, trussed with black floss. Trim ends to make cute little bangs.

8

project

What you need to get started:

Materials & Tools

- General Items on page 12
- Painting Items on page 13
- Acrylic paints: black; soft brown; dark pink; rose; turquoise
- Black craft wire
- Cream yarn for hair
- Decorative papers (3)
- Glossy wood-toned spray stain
- Lacy doily, 4" diameter
- Matte spray sealer
- Paintbrushes: flat; liner; round stencil
- Small sunflower button
- Tiny craft spading fork
- Twine
- Wooden hearts: 4" tall (2) for wings; 1½" tall predrilled (2) for shoes
- Wooden jumbo-sized craft sticks, ¾" x 6" (2)
- Wooden paddle, 18½" x 4½"
- Wooden spools, 1" diameter

How do I make legs for a paddle doll?

Legs for a paddle doll can be as simple as wooden craft sticks or fancier like this doll's legs. Six wooden spools have been painted to coordinate with her clothing. The spools are then attached to the paddle with craft wire. Wooden hearts with predrilled holes have been painted and attached for cute little shoes.

Primitive Angel

Here's how:

Creating the Doll

1. Using **Primitive Angel's Face** pattern on page 106, prepare pattern piece. Refer to **Preparing the Patterns** on page 16.

2. Prepare wood. Refer to **Preparing the Wood** on page 25. Using flat brush, base-coat paddle, craft sticks, and spools with soft brown paint. Let dry.

3. Paint small wooden hearts with turquoise paint.

4. Lightly sand all painted items.

5. Transfer eyes, nose, and mouth onto wood. Refer to **Transferring Facial Features onto Wood** on page 26.

6. Using stencil brush, dry-brush cheeks with rose paint. Refer to **Cheeks** on page 29.

7. Using liner brush, paint nose with black paint.

8. Paint mouth with rose paint. Refer to **Simple Lips** on page 31.

9. Using stylus, paint eyes with black paint. Refer to **Simple Eyes** on page 30.

10. Spray face and hands with sealer.

Continued on page 106.

Continued from page 104.

Dressing the Doll

1. Cover craft sticks with paper, leaving 3" at one end of each uncovered, for the hands. Refer to **Covering the Wood with Decorative Paper** on pages 25–26.

2. Using craft scissors, cut 4¼" x 5" from same paper used for sleeves. Adhere onto lower paddle.

3. Cut 4¼" x 12" from paper for apron, trim to fit upper body. Adhere onto paddle

4. Using fabric scissors, cut doily in half. Adhere onto shoulders. Adhere button to center of collar.

Creating a Hairdo

1. Make a pom-pom from yarn. Refer to **Embroidery Floss, Thread & Yarn** on page 33.

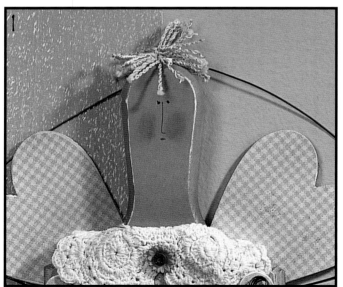

Assembling the Doll

1. Adhere wings to back of doll at a slight angle.

2. Attach arms and legs to body. Refer to **Securing Wooden Arms & Legs onto Body** on page 27.

Making a Hanger

1. Drill hole a 1½" from upper-right corner of dress. Repeat on upper-left corner.

2. Make a hanger. Refer to **Making a Hanger**, Steps 1b–1d on page 68.

Finishing the Doll

1. Spray sides and back of doll, as well as the flag, with wood-toned stain.

2. Cut 3" piece of twine. Tie twine around handle of spading fork.

3. Using glue gun, adhere twine to left hand.

> **Author's Tips:**
> - Use a different paddle such as a wider and shorter version.
> - Paint the handle for the head and use bright spring colors of decorative paper for the body.
> - Use square wooden cubes instead of wooden spools for the legs. It will give the doll a completely different look.

Pattern for Primitive Angel

Primitive Angel's Face

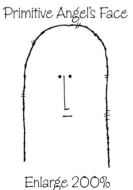

Enlarge 200%

Spooky Witch
(Variation of Primitive Angel)

Using the same methods that were used for Primitive Angel on pages 104–106, create this Spooky Witch. Adhere a small nose, made from from ⅛" dowel cut to ⅜", onto a wooden paddle. Paint her face and hands pale green.

Adhere a small witch hat that can be purchased at most craft stores. Adhere a bewitching tulle scarf embellished with moons and stars around her neck and down the front. Make her clothing from decorative paper. Her legs are made from small wooden spools and wooden moons painted to match her clothing. Refer to **Securing Wooden Arms & Legs onto Body** page 27.

9
project

What you need to get started:

Materials & Tools
- General Items on page 12
- Painting Items on page 13
- Acrylic paints: black; dark blue; burnt umber; light cream; light green; red; sand; light tan; terra-cotta
- Black felt cowboy hat
- Buttons (3)
- Coping saw
- Christmas tree button
- Cream yarn scraps for hair
- Extra-fine iridescent glitter
- Fabric or ribbon scrap for scarf
- Jute twine
- Matte spray sealer
- Paintbrushes: flat; liner; round stencil
- Pencil sharpener
- Wooden dowel, ¼" diameter
- Wooden mittens, 2" (2)
- Wooden paddle board, 18½" x 4½"

How do I use special painting methods on a paddle doll?

If you liked the other paddle dolls, but wish there was more painting technique, this is the doll for you. The Little Snowman includes such techniques as dry-brushing, floating and using a stylus to apply paint. Little bits of fabric, a little felt hat, and wooden mittens complete his wardrobe.

Little Snowman

Here's how:
Creating the Doll

1. Using **Little Snowman's Face** pattern on opposite, prepare pattern piece. Refer to **Preparing the Patterns** on page 16.

2. Prepare wood. Refer to **Preparing the Wood** on page 25. Using flat brush, base-coat paddle with dark blue paint. Let dry.

3. Sand lightly and coat with sand paint, leaving some of blue peeking through.

4. Using stencil brush, dry-brush center area with light cream paint, then edges with tan paint. Refer to **Cheeks** on page 29.

5. Using flat brush, float edges with burnt-umber paint. Refer to **Floating Method** on page 28.

6. Transfer facial details onto paddle. Refer to **Transferring Facial Features onto Wood** on page 26. Do not transfer the dotted lines on pattern onto wooden paddle.

7. Make nose by sharpening one end of dowel with pencil sharpener, then use a coping saw to cut off pointed end. *Note: If you don't have a coping saw, you can sometimes use a sharp pair of wire cutters, but you need to sand end so it is flat enough to adhere onto face.*

8. Paint nose with terra-cotta paint. Sand lightly and adhere onto face.

9. Using stencil brush, dry-brush cheeks with red paint.

10. Using stylus, apply dots for eyes and mouth with black paint. Refer to **Simple Eyes** on page 30.

11. Paint mittens with light green paint. Paint cuffs with red paint. Using stylus, apply light cream dots on cuffs.

Creating a Hairdo

1. Make a tiny pom-pom with yarn for hair. Refer to **Embroidery Floss, Thread & Yarn** on page 33.

2. Using your fingers, push out crease from top of cowboy hat and place onto top of head to determine placement of hairdo. Using craft glue, adhere pom-pom.

3. Using glue gun, adhere hat onto top of head.

Dressing the Doll

1. Tear a 1"-wide strip from desired fabric for scarf. Tie strip around neck, varying length of scarf ends.

2. Using glue gun, adhere buttons down front and Christmas tree button to scarf.

3. Using craft scissors, cut 15" length of jute. Adhere mittens over raw ends of jute. Place jute around neck, dangling down the front.

4. Spray with sealer, and while still wet, sprinkle fine glitter over doll and clothing.

Pattern for Little Snowman

Little Snowman Face

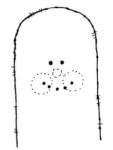

Enlarge 200%

About the Author

Miriam Gourley was born in Colorado, back in the '50s. She was the eldest of eight children—four girls and four boys. They lived on a ranch. Her father was a carpenter/rancher and her mother had Art and English degrees; so between the two of them, they all grew up with a love for making things. Miriam learned to sew on her mother's old Singer treadle machine, which her mother still uses. Miriam and her sister learned to stitch wonderful Barbie clothes and house decorations.

About twenty years ago, she was introduced to a woman who was making her own patterns and selling them. She was intrigued by the idea, and planned for and attended her first Quilt Market with this woman. They both enjoyed moderate success and kept attending, eventually meeting their friends from Ogden, from a designer firm then called The Vanessa-Ann Collection. They and many others inspired and taught Miriam , as she explored her way into a design career.

Miriam has since been published by Oxmoor House, *Better Homes and Gardens, Woman's Day, Crafts Magazine, The Quilt Digest Press*, Sterling Publishing, and others. She does freelance work for several fabric vendors, including Fabric Country and Michael Miller. She has coproduced a special for public television and has been a guest on several cable shows. She is one of three designers who work for a local retail craft store, creating displays.

Miriam is also the mother of four children—three boys and one daughter. Of all the things she has helped to create, they are the best and most satisfying.

Acknowledgments

A special thank-you to Suzy Skadburg and to Dave and Debbie Spilker for allowing us to photograph parts of this book in their homes. Their trust and cooperation are greatly appreciated.

A special thanks to Wayne Frederick Christensen, my brother, for his photography. All the how-to shots were carefully lighted and photographed by Wayne, and the fact that he was able to work with my schedule so well enabled this aspect of the book production to be especially trouble-free.

Mary Thomas Brown is the illustrator, and has the uncanny ability to understand the various procedures and illustrate them with very little guidance. Her attitude has always been cheerful and helpful, and I appreciate her contribution to this book.

This book is dedicated to my sister Sonia, my favorite playmate yesterday and today.

Metric Equivalency Charts

mm-millimetres   cm-centimetres
inches to millimetres and centimetres

inches	mm	cm	inches	cm	inches	cm
⅛	3	0.3	9	22.9	30	76.2
¼	6	0.6	10	25.4	31	78.7
⅜	10	1.0	11	27.9	32	81.3
½	13	1.3	12	30.5	33	83.8
⅝	16	1.6	13	33.0	34	86.4
¾	19	1.9	14	35.6	35	88.9
⅞	22	2.2	15	38.1	36	91.4
1	25	2.5	16	40.6	37	94.0
1¼	32	3.2	17	43.2	38	96.5
1½	38	3.8	18	45.7	39	99.1
1¾	44	4.4	19	48.3	40	101.6
2	51	5.1	20	50.8	41	104.1
2½	64	6.4	21	53.3	42	106.7
3	76	7.6	22	55.9	43	109.2
3½	89	8.9	23	58.4	44	111.8
4	102	10.2	24	61.0	45	114.3
4½	114	11.4	25	63.5	46	116.8
5	127	12.7	26	66.0	47	119.4
6	152	15.2	27	68.6	48	121.9
7	178	17.8	28	71.1	49	124.5
8	203	20.3	29	73.7	50	127.0

yards to metres

yards	metres	yards	metres	yards	metres	yards	metres	yards	metres
⅛	0.11	2⅛	1.94	4⅛	3.77	6⅛	5.60	8⅛	7.43
¼	0.23	2¼	2.06	4¼	3.89	6¼	5.72	8¼	7.54
⅜	0.34	2⅜	2.17	4⅜	4.00	6⅜	5.83	8⅜	7.66
½	0.46	2½	2.29	4½	4.11	6½	5.94	8½	7.77
⅝	0.57	2⅝	2.40	4⅝	4.23	6⅝	6.06	8⅝	7.89
¾	0.69	2¾	2.51	4¾	4.34	6¾	6.17	8¾	8.00
⅞	0.80	2⅞	2.63	4⅞	4.46	6⅞	6.29	8⅞	8.12
1	0.91	3	2.74	5	4.57	7	6.40	9	8.23
1⅛	1.03	3⅛	2.86	5⅛	4.69	7⅛	6.52	9⅛	8.34
1¼	1.14	3¼	2.97	5¼	4.80	7¼	6.63	9¼	8.46
1⅜	1.26	3⅜	3.09	5⅜	4.91	7⅜	6.74	9⅜	8.57
1½	1.37	3½	3.20	5½	5.03	7½	6.86	9½	8.69
1⅝	1.49	3⅝	3.31	5⅝	5.14	7⅝	6.97	9⅝	8.80
1¾	1.60	3¾	3.43	5¾	5.26	7¾	7.09	9¾	8.92
1⅞	1.71	3⅞	3.54	5⅞	5.37	7⅞	7.20	9⅞	9.03
2	1.83	4	3.66	6	5.49	8	7.32	10	9.14

Index